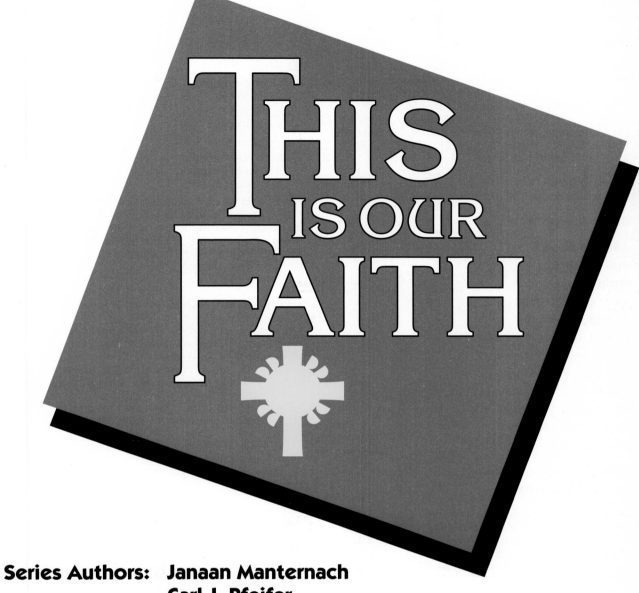

THIS IS OUR FAITH

Series Authors: **Janaan Manternach**
Carl J. Pfeifer

Authors: **Jeannine Wadoz Goggin**
Stephanie Spence, ANG
Maureen Gallagher
Joan R. DeMerchant
Jean Marie Weber

Contributing Author: **Kate Sweeney Ristow**

SILVER BURDETT GINN
PARSIPPANY, NJ

THIS IS OUR FAITH
SCHOOL PROGRAM

Contributing Authors: James Bitney, Robert Hamma, Paula A. Lenz, Judene Leon, Yvette Nelson, Sister Carolyn Puccio, C.S.J., Anna Ready, Kate Sweeney Ristow, Barbara Carol Vasiloff, Sister Maureen Shaughnessy, S.C., Sister Cecilia Maureen Cromwell, I.H.M., Patricia Frevert, Mary Lou Ihrig, Sister Arlene Pomije, C.S.J., Sister Mary Agnes Ryan, I.H.M., Brother Michael Sheerin, F.M.S.

Opening Doors: A Take-Home Magazine: Peter H.M. Demkovitz, Janie Gustafson, Margaret Savitskas

Day to Day: Skills for Christian Living: Susan G. Keys

Advisory Board:

Rev. Louis J. Cameli

Philip J. Cunningham

Sister Clare E. Fitzgerald

William J. Freburger

Greer J. Gordon

Sister Veronica R. Grover, S.H.C.J.

Rev. Thomas Guarino

Rev. Robert E. Harahan

Rev. Eugene LaVerdieré, S.S.S.

Rev. Frank J. McNulty

Rev. Msgr. John J. Strynkowski

National Catechical Advisor:

Kathleen Hendricks

Consultants: Linda Blanchette, Anita Bridge, Fred Brown, Rod Brownfield, Sister Mary Michael Burns, S.C., Pat Burns, Bernadine Carroll, Mary Ellen Cocks, Sister Peggy Conlon, R.S.M., Mary Ann Crowley, Pamela Danni, Sister Jamesetta DeFelice, O.S.U., Sister Mary Elizabeth Duke, S.N.D., Mary M. Gibbons, Yolanda Gremillion, Sister Angela Hallahan, C.H.F., Alice T. Heard, Sister Michele O'Connoll, P.B.V.M., Sister Angela O'Mahoney, P.B.V.M., Sister Ruthann O'Mara, S.S.J., Sandra Okulicz-Hulme, Judy Papandria, Rachel Pasano, Sallie Ann Phelan, Sister Geraldine M. Rogers, S.S.J., Mary Lou Schlosser, Patricia Ann Sibilia, Margaret E. Skelly, Lisa Ann Sorlie, Sister Victorine Stoltz, O.S.B., Sister Nancy Jean Turner, S.H.C.J., Christine Ward, Judith Reidel Weber, Kay White, Elizabeth M. Williams, Catherine R. Wolf, Florence Bambrick Yarney, Kathryn K. Zapcic

Nihil Obstat

Kathleen Flanagan, S.C., Ph.D.
Censor Librorum

Ellen Joyce, S.C., Ph.D.
Censor Librorum

Imprimatur

✠ Most Reverend Frank J. Rodimer
  Bishop of Paterson
  November 8, 1996

The *nihil obstat* and *imprimatur* are official declarations that a book or pamphlet is free of doctrinal and moral error. No implication is contained therein that those who have granted the *nihil obstat* and *imprimatur* agree with the contents, opinions, or statements expressed.

ACKNOWLEDGMENTS

Scriptural texts used in this work are taken from the *New American Bible with Revised New Testament*, Copyright © 1970, 1986 by the Confraternity of Christian Doctrine, Washington, DC, and are used by permission of copyright owner. All rights reserved.

All adaptations of Scripture are based on *the New American Bible with Revised New Testament*.

"Blessings of a Pet" reprinted with permission from the *New St. Joseph's People's Prayer Book* (page 1037), copyright © 1980 by Catholic Book Publishing Co., New York, NY. All rights reserved.

Excerpts from the English translation of *Rite of Baptism for Children* © 1969, International Committee on English in the Liturgy, Inc. (ICEL); excerpts from the English translation of *Rite of Christian Initiation of Adults* © 1988, ICEL; excerpts from the English translation of *The Roman Missal* © 1973, ICEL; excerpts from the English translation of *Rite of Penance* © 1974, ICEL; excerpts from the English translation of *Rite of Confirmation*, Second Edition © 1975, ICEL; excerpts from the English translation of *Pastoral Care of the Sick: Rites of Anointing and Viaticum* © 1982, ICEL; excerpts from the English translation of Eucharistic Prayers for Masses with Children © 1975, ICEL. All rights reserved.

6 7 8 9 10–W–05 04 03 02 01 00 99

Contents 〰〰〰

LET US PRAY

Let Us Pray

Sign of the Cross

In the name of the Father,
  and of the Son,
  and of the Holy Spirit.
Amen.

The Lord's Prayer

Our Father, who art
  in heaven,
    hallowed be thy name;
thy kingdom come;
thy will be done on earth
    as it is in heaven.
Give us this day
  our daily bread;
and forgive us
    our trespasses
    as we forgive those
    who trespass against us;
and lead us not
    into temptation,
    but deliver us from evil.
Amen.

Hail Mary

Hail Mary, full of grace,
 the Lord is with you.
Blessed are you among
 women,
 and blessed is the fruit
 of your womb, Jesus.
Holy Mary,
 Mother of God,
 pray for us sinners,
 now, and at the hour
 of our death.
Amen.

Glory Be to the Father

Glory be to the Father,
 and to the Son,
 and to the Holy Spirit.
As it was in the
 beginning, is now,
 and ever shall be,
 world without end.
Amen.

Let Us Pray

A Morning Prayer
My God, I offer you today
    all I think and do and say,
    uniting it with what was
    done on earth,
    by Jesus Christ, your Son.
Amen.

Evening Prayer
Dear God, before I sleep
    I want to thank you
    for this day
    so full of your kindness
    and your joy.
I close my eyes to rest safe
    in your loving care.
Amen.

Grace Before Meals

Bless us, O Lord, and these your gifts,
   which we are about to receive
   from your goodness,
   through Christ our Lord.
Amen.

Grace After Meals

We give you thanks for all your gifts,
   almighty God,
   living and reigning
   now and forever.
Amen.

Let Us Pray

Prayer to My Guardian Angel

Angel of God, my guardian dear,
   to whom God's love commits me here.
Ever this day be at my side
   to light and guard, to rule and guide.
Amen.

Prayer of Sorrow

My God,
I am sorry for my sins with all my heart.
In choosing to do wrong
and failing to do good,
I have sinned against you
whom I should love above all things.
I firmly intend, with your help,
to do penance,
to sin no more,
and to avoid whatever
leads me to sin.
Our Savior Jesus Christ
suffered and died for us.
In his name, my God,
have mercy.
Revised Rite of Penance

Beginning the Journey

We are starting a journey. Where are we going on our journey? Who will go with us?

My teacher's name is

_____

- -

_____

Many children will go with me on the journey. Here are some of their names.

_____

- -

_____

_____

- -

_____

_____

- -

_____

My family will join me on this journey, too. Here is a picture of my family.

Prayer for the Journey

Leader: We begin our journey with prayer. In the name of the Father, and of the Son, and of the Holy Spirit.

All: Amen.

Leader: God, you care for us like a loving father. Be with us as we begin our journey. Help us to be good friends and followers of Jesus, your Son.

All: Amen.

Leader: The Bible is a very special book. It is a holy book. Through the words of the Bible, God speaks to us. In the Bible, Jesus says, "Come, follow me. I am the way. I will lead you to life and happiness. Walk in my light. I will be with you." [pause] The gospel of the Lord.

All: Praise to you, Lord Jesus Christ.

Leader: Let us now show that we want to start on our journey to know and love Jesus better by signing our names on the inside front cover of our books.

THIS IS OUR FAITH

✦ A Preview of Grade **2**

You are cordially invited...

A Profile of the Second-Grade Child

No one knows your seven-year-old better than you! It may be helpful and interesting to you as a parent or guardian, however, to explore some of the characteristics of the second grader.

Second Graders

- are active.
- are inquisitive.
- are full of life.
- are more sure of themselves.
- are still dependent on the guidance of their parents, teachers, and other adults.
- need activities of short duration, perhaps no more than eight to ten minutes.
- need a variety of different kinds of activities.
- learn best when involved in doing something, such as drawing or singing.

- need to be involved in real objects and experiences.
- need lots of reminders.
- need to experience success at simple tasks.
- need acceptance of their feelings of joy, fear, sadness, and anger.
- need to be encouraged to share.
- need a model of someone who shares.
- think more easily about the concrete (a peanut butter and jelly sandwich) than about the abstract (nutrition).

THIS IS OUR FAITH Grade 2 Program has been designed to reflect the doctrine presented in the *Catechism of the Catholic Church* at a level that is appropriate for the second-grade child.

to continue in faith the same journey you first embarked on the day you presented your son or daughter for Baptism. Throughout the years you have been and continue to be the most important person of faith for your child. As your second-grader commits to this year's faith journey, you are invited as the primary educator in faith to journey along with your child, in whatever way is most comfortable for you. This Is Our Faith is privileged to assist you in this important task.

This Year in Grade 2

This year your second grader will be introduced to some of the basic teachings about the sacramental life of the Catholic Church as he or she discovers what it means to belong to the Christian community.

In Unit 1 your child will be reminded of the communities to

which he or she belongs: your family, your town, your school, and your parish. This first unit will remind your child that we respond to our membership in the Catholic Church by embracing Jesus' values and teachings and by accepting our responsibilities as members of this community.

As your child completes each unit of This Is Our Faith, you will receive a take-home magazine entitled, Opening Doors: A Take-Home Magazine. Each magazine will include the following features to help you grow in your own faith and to help you share that faith with your child.

OPENING DOORS
A Take-Home Magazine™

A Closer Look

includes an article relating the unit theme to a particular aspect of the Mass and family interactive pages for you and your child to enjoy together.

Being Catholic

highlights a particular aspect of our Catholic heritage.

Growing Closer

suggests activities to help you and your family integrate your faith into everyday life.

And also . . .

Looking Ahead

previews the next unit of This Is Our Faith.

UNIT 1

Our Church Celebrates Sacraments

What is your favorite celebration?

We Belong to the Catholic Church

What is the name of a group of people you like to do things with?

A Group of Friends

As I was walking to the park,
I met a boy whose name was Mark.
I asked him, "Would you like to play?"
He smiled and said, "Well, yes! Okay."

We played that day and many more.
Then two more joined, and now we're four.
Different, yet the same are we,
We have all become a group you see,
A group that is **community**.

Jesus Calls Us to Be Friends

Jesus calls us to be friends with each other and with him. Friends and followers of Jesus are called **Christians**.

Jesus also calls us to be a **community**. A community is a group of people who shares something important together.

We belong to the Christian community called the **Catholic Church**. The Catholic Church shares our **faith** in Jesus.

Activity

Fill in the name of the Catholic Church where you and your family share faith.

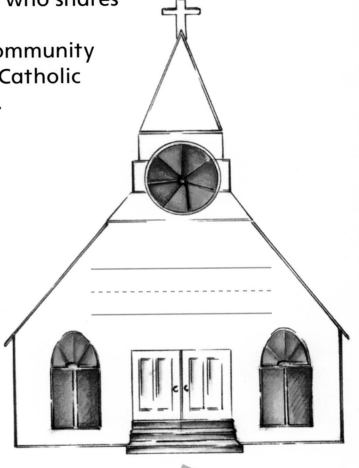

New Words

Christians	friends and followers of Jesus Christ
community	a group of people who share something important together
Catholic Church	the Christian community to which we belong
faith	faith in Jesus means that we have come to know him and trust him.

We Believe

We are friends and followers of Jesus Christ. We belong to the Christian community called the Catholic Church.

Walk with Me

One day, Jesus was walking along the seashore. He stopped to watch two men who were fishing with a net. The fishermen's names were Peter and Andrew. Jesus went over to talk with them.

"Come with me," Jesus said to them. "I want you to be my followers."

Jesus continued walking along the seashore. Peter and Andrew decided to walk with him.

Jesus saw two other fishermen, James and John. They were sitting in their boat. James and John were fixing their nets.

"Come," Jesus called to them.
"Be my followers. Walk with me."
So James and John joined Jesus,
Peter, and Andrew. Together they
walked and talked on the shore.
They became friends.

Based on Matthew 4:18–22

Activity

1. Circle three things you like to talk about when you walk with your friends.

   my family   games and sports   school

   my favorite things   my pets   my friends

2. Name something you think Jesus and his friends talked about.

   _____

   _

   _____

3. Jesus and his friends formed a

   _____

   _

   _____ .

Discovering Our Parish

Catholics gather together in communities called **parishes**. The leader of a parish is called a **pastor**. There is usually more than one Catholic parish in a large town or city. Can you name another Catholic parish that you have visited?

Maria Explores Her Parish Church

1. "This **parish church** is a special place, where the people of God meet," Dad said.

   "This font of water is called the **baptismal font**," Maria said. "This is where the new members of the Church are baptized."

2. "And this is the **altar**," Dad said. "The altar is a table where the second part of the Mass is celebrated."

3. "This is called the **ambo**," Dad told Maria. "This is where the word of God is read and explained."

4. "I know what this is!" Maria said with excitement. "This is a **crucifix**. It's Jesus' cross." Maria and Dad prayed a quiet prayer and then walked home.

New Words

Catholics	followers of Jesus who belong to the Catholic Church
parish	another name for our Christian community
pastor	the leader of a parish
parish church	a place where Catholics gather to pray with other members of the Catholic Church
baptismal font	the water font where new members of the Church are baptized
altar	the table at which the Mass is celebrated
ambo	the reading stand where the word of God is read
crucifix	a cross that holds the body of Jesus

Special Objects Used at Mass

A sacristy is a small room inside a church where the objects that are used during Mass are kept.

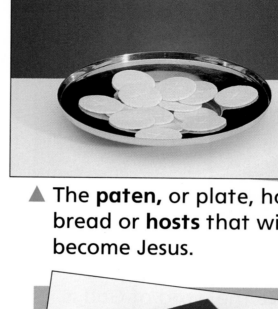

▲ The **paten,** or plate, holds bread or **hosts** that will become Jesus.

▲ **Vestments** are the special garments the priest wears during Mass.

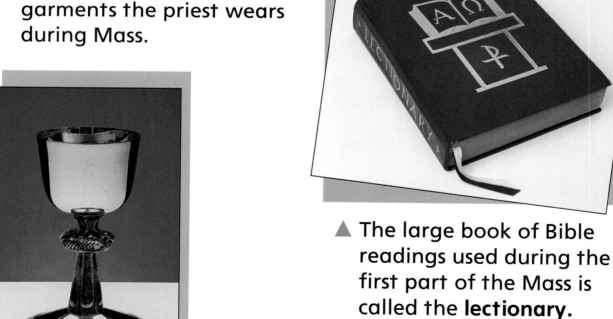

▲ The large book of Bible readings used during the first part of the Mass is called the **lectionary.**

◀ The **chalice,** or cup, holds the wine that will become Jesus.

Activity

Draw a picture of one special object that you have discovered in your church. Then tell the story of how it is used.

New Words

vestments	special garments worn by the priest during Mass
paten	the plate that holds the bread or hosts at Mass
hosts	bread that becomes the Body of Christ at Mass
lectionary	the book where all the Bible readings used at Mass are found
chalice	the cup that holds the wine at Mass

Praying in the Presence of God

Teacher: God is here in this church. We light a candle to remember that God is with us. There are many other things that remind us that God is present. Now let us pray a song of praise.

All: Holy, holy, holy Lord, God of power and might.

Teacher: God is also present in each one of us.
(Name), God lives in you.

Each child: Amen!

Teacher: Let us go forth from this holy place and live as God's holy people. We remember that God calls us sons and daughters. Let us live together in peace. Let us love one another.

All: Amen!

Chapter Review

Use the clues to fill in the crossword puzzle.

Down

1. Our special sign is the _____ .

2. We _____ to God, our Father.

Across

1. Catholics _____ about and love everyone in the world.

2. Our parish is a community of _____ who belong to the Catholic Church.

1. What do we call a group of people who share something important together?

   _____

   -

   _____

2. To which Christian community do we belong?

   _____

   -

   _____

3. Talk about something we do that shows we are Catholic Christians.

Jesus says,
"I want you to love one another as I love you."
Based on John 15:14

2

What are some ways you and your family celebrate people and things that are important to you?

We Celebrate Special Times

Celebrations

Almost everyone celebrates special people or special times. It is good to be together when we are happy and when we are sad. We sometimes use special actions, sing special songs, eat special foods, or wear special clothes when we celebrate. **Celebrations** are important times of being together.

What are the people in the photographs celebrating? What special actions, signs, and words are they using?

Activity

Draw a picture of you celebrating a special day.

Signs of Celebration

Some celebrations help us feel special. Some celebrations help us remember someone who is important to us. Most celebrations help us feel that we belong to each other.

We are also invited to take part in celebrations that use special signs to celebrate Jesus' friendship and **presence** with us. We call these special signs and celebrations the **seven sacraments**.

We Believe

Catholics have special signs and celebrations called the seven sacraments. Sacraments are signs and celebrations of Jesus' love for us that make him present to us now.

New Words

celebrations	special times of being together to show how important someone or something is to us
presence	being with someone
seven sacraments	special signs and celebrations of Jesus' love for us that make him present to us now

A Sign of Love

One day, Jesus visited his friends Martha, Mary, and Lazarus. They were glad to see Jesus and prepared a special meal to celebrate his visit. Martha, Mary, Lazarus, and some other guests sat with Jesus at the table.

After the meal, Mary showed her love for Jesus in a special way. She brought out some expensive perfume and poured it over the feet of Jesus. Then she dried his feet with her hair.

Another guest saw what Mary had done. He got very angry. "She could have sold the perfume for a lot of money," said the guest. "Instead, she wasted it."

Jesus replied, "Leave Mary alone. She is not wasting her gift. **Anointing** me with perfume is a sign of her love for me. She is celebrating my being here."

Based on John 12:1–8

Activity

If Jesus was coming to your home today, what would your special celebration look like? Draw a picture of your special celebration.

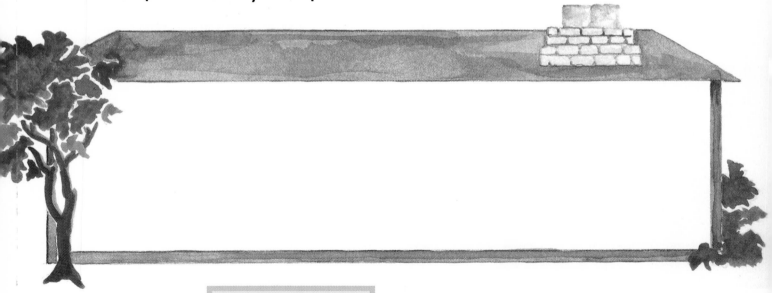

New Word

★
★
★ anointing   putting blessed oil on a person's body as a sign
★   of love, respect, honor, or healing
★

Celebrations of God's Love

Jesus is with us every day and in many different ways. Catholics also have special ways of being with Jesus. We call these celebrations the seven sacraments.

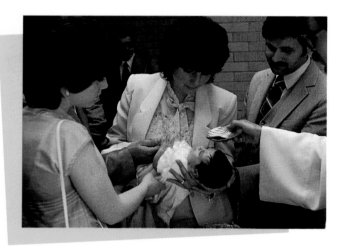

◀ Baptism is a sacrament that joins us to Jesus and welcomes us into the Church. We are baptized with water. Water is a sign that we share Jesus' new life.

In the sacrament of ▶ Confirmation, we receive the Holy Spirit in a special way. The Holy Spirit helps us to tell everyone the good news about Jesus.

◀ At Mass we share a special meal with Jesus. The Eucharist is another sacrament of Jesus' love.

◀ In the sacrament of Reconciliation, we say we are sorry for our sins. We celebrate God's forgiveness.

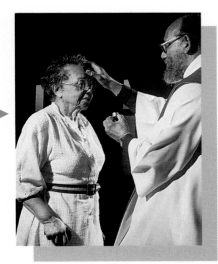

In Anointing of the Sick, ▶ Jesus brings his peace and help to people who are sick.

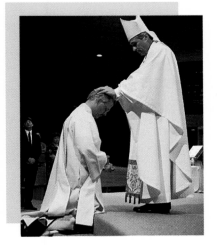

◀ In the sacrament of Holy Orders, men become deacons, priests, and bishops. They join Jesus' work in a special way.

In the sacrament of ▶ Matrimony or Marriage, a man and a woman promise to love each other. They celebrate their love in this sacrament.

Activity

Which sacrament have you already celebrated?

_____

- -

_____

Friends and Disciples

Some of Jesus' first friends were called **disciples**. They traveled together and ate meals together. They celebrated happy times together. They prayed together. The disciples learned many important things from Jesus.

Jesus' disciples told other people about Jesus. They taught others the same important things that Jesus had taught them.

Jesus invites us to be his disciples, too. He asks us to celebrate with others. He asks us to pray with each other and to listen to each other. Whenever we live and love like Jesus, we are being his disciples.

Activity

Circle some of the ways you can be a disciple of Jesus. Draw a line through actions that show how a person is not trying to be a disciple.

I can celebrate happy times with others.

I can be selfish with my toys.

I can invite friends to play with me.

I can fight with my brothers and sisters.

I can forgive someone who hurts me.

What Can You Do?

In the seven sacraments, we celebrate the special ways that Jesus is with us. We can become signs of Jesus' love when we show love to others. We show our love for other people by doing special things for them. What we do is a sign of our love.

Read the story below each picture. Talk about all the things you could do to show your love.

1. Your grandmother lives far away. You haven't seen her all summer. She is coming to visit tomorrow.

2. You have a friend who helps you. This friend is always there to play and talk with. Next week is your friend's birthday.

New Word

★
★
★ **disciples** people who live and love as Jesus did

Praying in Celebration of God's Love

Teacher: We gather to sing praise to our God.
Play beautiful melodies!

All: Sing a new song to the Lord!

Teacher: Sound the trumpets and horns!
Celebrate God with joyful songs.

All: Sing a new song to the Lord!

Teacher: Let the sea roar with its creatures.
Let the rivers clap their hands.

All: Sing a new song to the Lord!

Teacher: Let all the hills ring out their joy.
God loves us and all the earth.

All: Sing a new song to the Lord!

Teacher: Now let us praise God for the gift of
each other. We praise you, God, for
creating *(Name).*

All: Sing a new song to the Lord!

Based on Psalm 149

Chapter Review

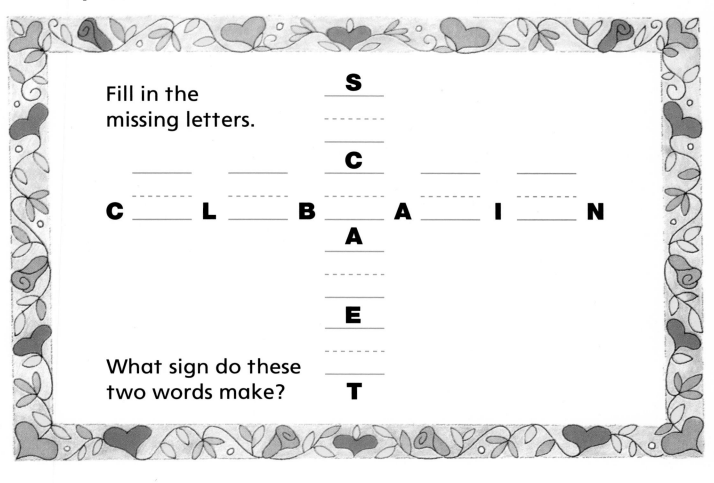

Fill in the
missing letters.

What sign do these
two words make?

```
                              S _____
                              - - - - -
                              C _____
C ___ L ___ B ___ A ___ I ___ N
                              A _____
                              - - - - -
                              E _____
                              - - - - -
                              T
```

1. What do we call a special time when we show how important someone or something is to us?

   _____

   -

   _____

2. What name do Catholics give to special celebrations of Jesus' love for us and our love for him?

   _____

   -

   _____

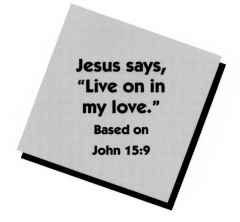

Jesus says,
"Live on in
my love."
Based on
John 15:9

3. Talk about what we can do to follow Jesus as his disciples.

We Celebrate Baptism

▲ What are the children doing that makes you feel they welcome one another?

What happens when we are welcomed into a group or family?

Come and Join Us

Say your name and where you live,
And promise, cross your heart,
That as a member of our group
You, too, will do your part.

And now that you have done all this,
We'll sing a welcome song.
For you are now a part of us,
To us you now belong.

Jesus Welcomes Us

Jesus told his disciples to tell others about him. He told his disciples to invite all people who love him into his community.

"Go out and welcome people of all nations," Jesus said to them. "Baptize them in the name of the Father, and of the Son, and of the Holy Spirit. Teach them all that I have taught you. And know that I am with you always."

Based on Matthew 28:18–20

Activity

Underline the things in the story that Jesus asks his followers to do.

Our Church Welcomes Us

Our Church welcomes new members at the sacrament of **Baptism**. At Baptism we become members of the Church and share new life with Jesus.

We Believe

The Catholic community welcomes new members at Baptism, and our lives are joined to Jesus. At Baptism, Jesus gives us new life, the life of the Holy Spirit. Baptism is one of the seven sacraments.

New Word

Baptism   Baptism is a sacrament of welcome. At Baptism, our lives are joined to Jesus and the Church welcomes us as new members.

Signs Are All Around Us

Our world is full of signs. There are signs that remind us of people and events. There are signs that remind us of special places and things.

Activity

Find your way to school by using the signs in the map below.

Go past the . At the corner, watch the 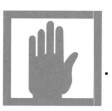.

You can safely cross the street when the  is lighted.

Next you'll pass the . Then you'll pass the

. You're almost there! Look up ahead. Do you

see the ? That's your school!

Signs of New Life

Just as there are signs all around us in our world, the sacrament of Baptism has signs, too. These signs remind us of our new life in Jesus.

◀ **Water**
The priest pours water over our heads to remind us that Baptism washes away our old life. We are now new people who live in Jesus' love.

◀ **White garment**
The garment reminds us that it is Jesus' new life we put on when we are baptized.

◀ **Oil**
At Baptism, we anoint the person's head with oil as a sign that God calls us to live special lives. We are called to live as Jesus lived.

▲ **Lighted candle**
We light a candle to remind us that Jesus is the Light of the World. A lighted candle is a sign of Baptism.

Mark's Baptism

as told by his sister, Lisa Ann

Today is a wonderful day for my family. My new baby brother, Mark, is being baptized at Sunday Mass. All of our family and friends are here. And so is the rest of our parish family.

1. Father Adams welcomes everyone, especially Mark. Then the Mass begins.

2. Soon it is time for Mark to be baptized. Father Adams makes the sign of the cross on Mark's head. Then Mom and Dad do the same. And so do Uncle Peter and Aunt Ruth, who are so proud to have been chosen to be Mark's **godparents**.

3. Father Adams asks everyone if we believe in God the Father, and in Jesus, and in the Holy Spirit. We all answer, "I do."

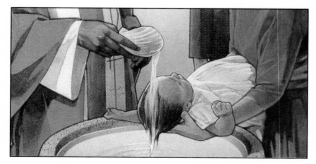

4. Father Adams pours water over Mark's head. He says, "I baptize you, Mark, in the name of the Father, and of the Son, and of the Holy Spirit."

5. Father Adams makes the sign of the cross on Mark's head with blessed oil. He puts a white robe on Mark. He prays that Mark will live as a friend of Jesus.

6. Mark looks up at the lighted candle. Father Adams says, "Mark, receive the light of Christ." Then he gives the special candle to Mom and Dad.

7. Father Adams blesses Mom and Dad. Then he blesses all of us. And that's when Mark falls asleep.

Activity

Color the signs of Baptism. Draw a line through the objects that are not signs of Baptism.

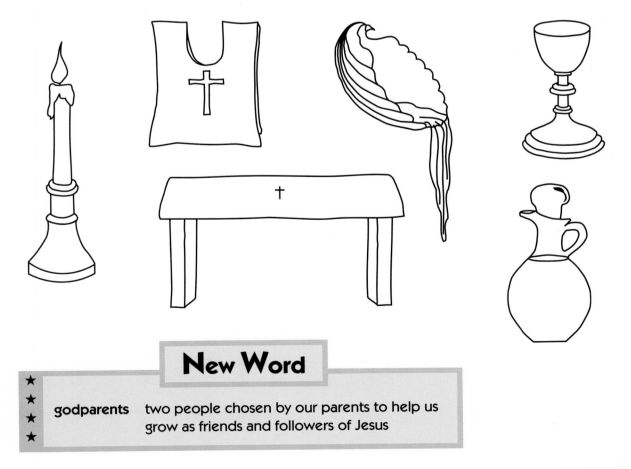

New Word

★
★
★
★   **godparents**   two people chosen by our parents to help us grow as friends and followers of Jesus

What We Believe

The Catholic Church welcomed us at Baptism. We celebrated becoming members of the Christian community.

At Baptism, the priest asked some questions and our parents and godparents answered for us. The priest asked them what they believed as Catholics. Here are some questions the priest asked. Now you can answer for yourself. Write the words **I do** in each speech balloon.

Do you believe in God, who made the world and everything in it?

Do you believe in Jesus Christ, the Son of God, our brother and friend?

Do you believe in the Holy Spirit, our helper and guide, and in the Catholic Church?

Activity

You are a member of the Catholic Church. Name something you now know about Jesus that you did not know when you were baptized.

_____

- -

_____

Then ask your family to help you complete this certificate.

My Baptism

My name is _____

I was baptized on _____

                (month)   (day)   (year)

My godmother is _____

My godfather is _____

Praying with Water and the Cross

Teacher: Let us gather together around this candle in the name of Jesus, in whom we are baptized.

Teacher: We have been signed with the waters of Baptism. Let us remember our new life in Jesus by marking ourselves with water and the cross.

All: Jesus, we are happy to be called your friends. Thank you for welcoming us into the Christian community through the waters of Baptism. Amen.

WE BELONG TO JESUS!

Chapter Review

Circle signs of new life that we see at Baptism.

oil

water

table

lighted candle

food

window

fish

white garment

1. What do we call the first sacrament of welcome into the Christian community that joins our lives with Jesus?

   _____

   -

   _____

2. What does Jesus give us at Baptism?

   _____

   -

   _____

Welcome one another just as Jesus welcomes you.
Based on
Romans 15:7

3. Talk about what happens at a Baptism that makes it a special celebration for each of us.

4

We Celebrate Confirmation

Miguel Feels More Welcomed

How do you make someone feel welcomed to your home or to your group of friends?

Miguel wanted to join the Cub Scouts. The first time he went to a meeting he felt afraid because he did not know anyone in the troop.

The scoutmaster welcomed Miguel warmly. He introduced him to the troop. By the end of the meeting, Miguel began to feel welcomed.

"You need to learn the Cub Scout promise before the next meeting," the scoutmaster told him. "If you can say it at the next meeting, you'll receive your uniform."

Miguel studied the promise. He said it over and over to anyone who would listen.

The night of the meeting finally came. Now it was Miguel's turn to say the promise.

"Are you ready, Miguel?" the scoutmaster asked.

"I sure am!" Miguel responded.

Miguel recited the promise without any mistakes. The other scouts cheered. The scoutmaster congratulated Miguel and gave him his uniform.

Everyone was very proud of Miguel.

Welcomed Again

When most of us were babies, our parish community welcomed us at Baptism. We are welcomed again as members of the Church in the sacrament of **Confirmation**. The Holy Spirit promises to make us strong in faith. We share the gifts of the Holy Spirit with others.

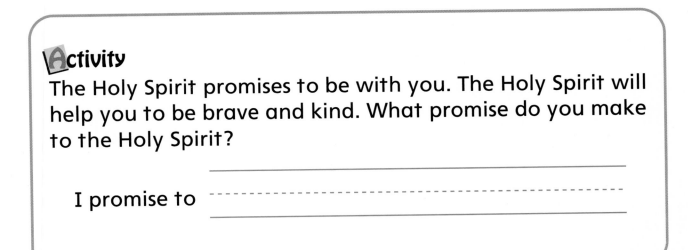

Activity

The Holy Spirit promises to be with you. The Holy Spirit will help you to be brave and kind. What promise do you make to the Holy Spirit?

I promise to _____

New Word

Confirmation   Confirmation is another sacrament of welcome into the Catholic Church through which the Holy Spirit makes us strong to live and share our faith in Jesus.

Activity

Everyone is afraid of something. Name something that frightens you.

_____

- -

_____

The Disciples Receive the Holy Spirit

The disciples of Jesus were afraid because Jesus was no longer with them. They hid in an upper room. Suddenly they heard a noise, like a strong wind blowing. Tongues of fire appeared over each of them. The **Holy Spirit** filled them with courage. They began to speak in many languages. They told the people to believe in Jesus.

Based on Acts 2:1–4

Signs of Confirmation

Jesus sent the Holy Spirit to his disciples to help make them strong. The Holy Spirit can help us become strong friends and followers of Jesus.

At Confirmation we celebrate the presence of the Holy Spirit. The signs below remind us that the Holy Spirit comes to us in this sacrament.

With hands stretched out, ▶ the bishop and priest pray to the Holy Spirit. They ask the Holy Spirit to help us and **guide** us. This sign is called the laying on of hands.

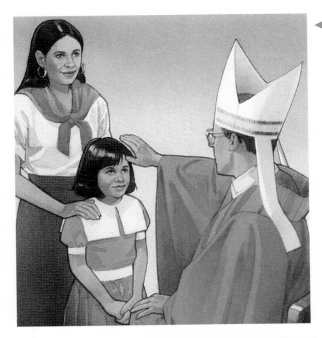

◀ The bishop anoints our foreheads with blessed oil. The bishop says, "Be sealed with the Gift of the Holy Spirit." That means "May you be filled with God's Spirit." Anointing with oil is another sign of Confirmation.

We Believe

Confirmation is another sacrament of welcome into the Catholic Church. We believe that the Holy Spirit is God's Spirit. The Holy Spirit helps us to follow Jesus and live holy lives.

New Words

★
★
★ **Holy Spirit** the Spirit of God who helps us follow Jesus
★
★ **guide** to show the way
★

Maria's Confirmation

as told by her brother, Alex

1. Father Adams presented Maria and her friends to the bishop. "Welcome," Bishop Lee said. "Today God will send the Holy Spirit to you in the sacrament of Confirmation. The Holy Spirit will unite you more closely with Jesus and with all his friends and followers."

2. Then the bishop asked Maria and the others to please stand. He asked, "Do you believe in God the Father, Jesus, and the Holy Spirit?" Each of them answered, "I do." Then Bishop Lee sprinkled them with holy water to remind them of their Baptism.

3. Bishop Lee and Father Adams stretched out their hands over Maria and the others being confirmed. They prayed that the Holy Spirit would make them stronger friends and followers of Jesus.

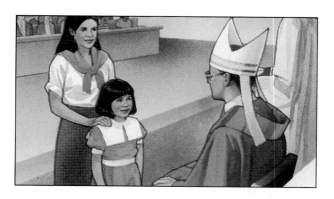

4. Then Maria and Mrs. Lopez, Maria's **sponsor**, stood before the bishop. Mrs. Lopez placed her hand on Maria's shoulder and told Bishop Lee that Maria had chosen Angela as her Confirmation name.

5. Bishop Lee dipped his thumb into a dish of blessed oil. Then he put his hand on Maria's head and made the sign of the cross on her forehead with his thumb. As he anointed her forehead, he said, "Angela, be sealed with the Gift of the Holy Spirit." She answered, "Amen."

6. The celebration did not end at church. Everyone went home and had a wonderful party.

Activity

Unscramble the words. Then write them on the lines below.

yaM   oyu   eb   flledi   ithw   'sdGo   Siprit

_____

- -

_____

- -

_____

New Word

★
★
★   **sponsor**   someone we choose at Confirmation to help us
★   live as a friend and follower of Jesus
★

Martin Learns to Help Others

Martin celebrated Confirmation this year. Martin decided to do something good for others. He knew that his younger sister, Meg, and her friends had no place to play. Martin felt bad but didn't know what he could do about it. Then Martin had an idea!

The next afternoon, Martin asked his friends to help him clean up the empty lot near their apartment house. It took a long time for Martin and his friends to pick up all the cans, broken glass, and garbage, but they didn't give up. They also cleaned the walls that were covered with spray paint.

Soon the little children had a safe and clean place to play. Meg and her friends were so happy. Martin was happy, too! The Holy Spirit gave Martin and his friends the strength to do something good for their neighborhood.

With the Holy Spirit's Help

The Holy Spirit helped Martin know what he could do to help others. The Holy Spirit helps those who are confirmed live as Christians. We pray to the Holy Spirit to give us the strength to do the right thing. Our Christian community will help us as we make our world a better place in which to live.

ctivity

What do you see the people doing that shows they are followers of Jesus?

Praying to the Holy Spirit

Teacher: Children, let us gather around this candle. Today we celebrate God's Spirit, the Holy Spirit.

Teacher: When we wake up in the morning...

All: Holy Spirit, fill our hearts with joy.

Teacher: When we learn new things...

All: Holy Spirit, fill our hearts with joy.

Teacher: When we play with our friends...

All: Holy Spirit, fill our hearts with joy.

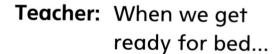

Teacher: When we get ready for bed...

All: Holy Spirit, fill our hearts with joy.

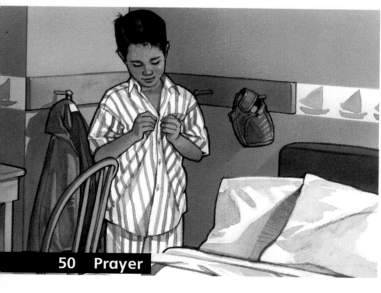

Chapter Review

Draw yourself doing something that shows you are a Catholic Christian, a friend and follower of Jesus.

1. What is another sacrament of welcome in which God sends us the Holy Spirit to make us strong friends and followers of Jesus?

2. At Confirmation, whom do we choose to help us live as friends and followers of Jesus?

3. Talk about what happens at Confirmation that makes us feel even more a part of the Catholic community.

"You are signed with the seal of the Holy Spirit."
Based on Ephesians 1:13

Start Unit **1** Organizer

Some communities I belong to are
_____
_____
_____
_____

Three of the seven sacraments are
_____
_____
_____
_____
_____

_____

_____

Baptism has special signs. Here is a picture of them.

Some important words about the sacrament of Confirmation are

Unit 1 Review

Choose a word in the box to finish each sentence. Write the word on the line below the sentence.

> Catholic   Christians   community
>
> Confirmation   sacraments

1. Followers of Jesus are called _____ .

2. We belong to the Christian community called the _____ Church.

3. Special signs and celebrations of Jesus' love for us that make him present to us now are called _____ .

4. Another sacrament of welcome is called _____ .

Unit 1 Review

5. Think about the story "Mark's Baptism." Number the pictures in the right order. Use the numbers **1** through **5**.

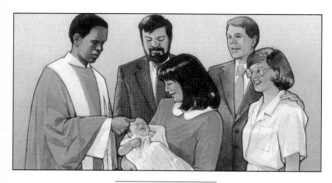

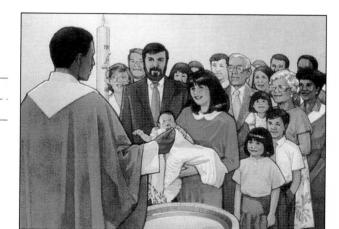

BEING A GOOD LISTENER

A good listener tunes in to the person who is speaking. What's wrong with the two pictures at the top of the page?

How can I tune in to someone who is speaking?

I can tune in to the person who is speaking by using eye contact, by paying attention, and by being quiet.

Activity

Draw a picture of you tuning in to someone who is speaking.

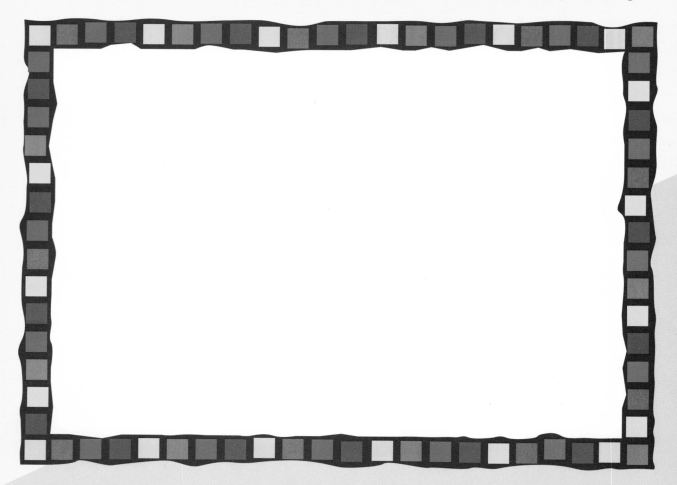

Being a good listener shows respect
for the person who is speaking.

Following Jesus

Jesus asks us to care about each other. Listening to someone is a special way to say, "I care about you." By being a good listener, I show care for the other person.

A Prayer

Jesus, you always listened well to others. Help us to be good listeners, too. Help us show our care for others by listening carefully to one another. Amen.

OPENING DOORS

A Take-Home Magazine™

THIS IS OUR FAITH

Growing Closer

A FAMILY COAT-OF-ARMS is a symbol of what makes a family special. Your family is special, too! Make a family coat-of-arms. Draw a symbol of your family. Then ask your family to add their own symbols.

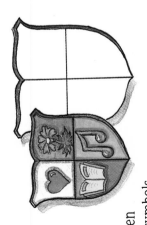

EVERYONE LIKES TO LOOK at family photos! Ask your family to look at photos with you. Remember that photos remind us of special people, places, and times. Enjoy this special time with your family!

Looking Ahead

Unit 2 will focus on the process of reconciliation. In the Scripture story of the Prodigal Son, the children will learn that God will always forgive us when we are sorry. And we, in turn, are called to forgive others. As Catholics we can celebrate God's forgiveness in a special way in the sacrament of Reconciliation.

8   Answers for page 5: holy water, Baptism: Eucharist, Jesus: Bible, God; lighted candle, pray

parish community, you probably have some idea who the other parishioners are and where they live. But how much do you know about your Catholic brothers and sisters outside the parish?

According to the *1989 Official Catholic Directory*, there are 54,918,989 Catholics in the United States today. This number makes up 22.48% of the total U.S. population. These Catholics live in 34 archdioceses and 154 dioceses throughout the country.

If you look at the chart, you will see how many Catholics live in each state and what percentage of the state's total population is Catholic.

State	Total Pop.	Catholic Pop.	Cath. %
Missouri	4,954,295	788,048	16
Montana	766,553	130,194	17
Nebraska	1,567,902	329,925	21
Nevada	1,002,570	147,000	15
New Hampshire	1,027,008	295,930	29
New Jersey	7,595,800	3,072,758	40
New Mexico	1,543,585	459,8683	30
New York	18,047,118	6,771,854	38
North Carolina	6,230,946	140,288	2
North Dakota	677,689	173,436	26
Ohio	10,764,839	2,219,167	21
Oklahoma	3,106,100	143,226	5
Oregon	2,690,550	282,390	10
Pennsylvania	11,979,366	3,579,707	30
Rhode Island	986,000	625,170	63
South Carolina	3,425,000	75,382	2
South Dakota	698,316	146,906	21
Tennessee	4,745,400	127,220	3
Texas	16,621,406	3,227,019	19
Utah	1,678,000	69,944	4
Vermont	541,000	147,816	27
Virginia	5,856,990	347,490	6
Washington	4,400,826	434,606	10
West Virginia	1,919,000	107,379	6
Wisconsin	4,890,364	1,531,706	31
Wyoming	482,088	60,120	12

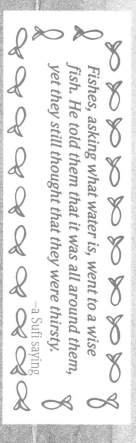

Fishes, asking what water is, went to a wise fish. He told them that it was all around them, yet they still thought that they were thirsty.

—a Sufi saying

The Sacred Around Us

From early on, we teach our children to make the sign of the cross, saying, "In the name of the Father, and of the Son, and of the Holy Spirit." It reminds us of the special nature of our Christian belief in the Trinity — three persons yet one God. We believe in a God who created us out of pure love that decided to share itself in abundance. We believe in a God who loved us so much that becoming one with us in Jesus was a complete expression of that love. We believe in a God who remains with us in the Spirit.

The sign of the cross also reminds us of one of our most distinctive characteristics as Catholics: our appreciation for and use of symbols.

Our faith gives us a kind of spiritual sight that transforms what we see and enables us to see more than the obvious. Symbols represent something beyond the obvious. (A cross is more than a horizontal and vertical beam; Eucharist, more than bread and wine.) Symbols also reveal, or make really present.

We believe, for example, that God's grace is revealed in the sacraments. We don't simply receive an explanation of what is represented in a sacrament. We experience and receive as gift the actual, or real presence of God in these special moments.

Why don't we always "see" it this way? For one reason or another, we all seem to forget at times that all life is sacred, that God is present everywhere. We know God's love through persons, places, events, nature, and even history. But we must make a deliberate choice to see our world in this way, through eyes of faith. And though faith is a gift, without the help of those special persons, places, and events in our lives that have helped us "see," we may never have recognized the gift.

Perhaps, then, the greatest gift we can give our children is the gift of a "sacra-mentality," a way of seeing and thinking that recognizes the sacred all around us.

Take the time to look around at the people in your home, at the people in church, at the movements and the actions of the various liturgical ministers at Mass. Take a good look at the symbols of our faith that reveal to us and to our children that indeed we live in a world of grace and that all of life is a gift that is ours to receive.

U.S. Catholics Today

In religious education classes, your child is being taught that the Catholic Church is a community — a group of people much like a family. Most families have a pretty good idea who the family members are and where they live. If you have participated for a while in your

Percentage of Catholics in U.S. Population

State	Total Pop.	Catholic Pop.	Cath. %
Alabama	3,464,335	126,774	4
Alaska	401,769	45,940	11
Arizona	3,121,200	577,920	19
Arkansas	2,360,000	69,416	3
California	27,538,436	6,137,006	22
Colorado	3,239,671	485,236	15
Connecticut	3,242,500	1,362,970	42
Delaware	814,300	134,598	17
District of Columbia	2,188,000	395,016	18
Florida	11,748,250	1,494,360	13
Georgia	6,630,555	216,368	3
Hawaii	1,062,344	191,520	18
Idaho	1,002,000	70,642	7
Illinois	11,490,981	3,535,524	31
Indiana	5,360,025	695,551	13
Iowa	2,895,039	510,388	18
Kansas	2,407,652	373,770	16
Kentucky	3,697,674	376,688	10
Louisiana	4,444,421	1,404,411	32
Maine	1,124,660	279,000	25
Maryland	2,508,947	438,016	17
Massachusetts	5,679,393	2,842,040	50
Michigan	9,010,107	2,281,181	25
Minnesota	4,072,371	1,097,821	27
Mississippi	2,548,981	99,197	4

Symbols All Around Us

Your child is already aware of many common symbols. Use the material on these two pages to help your child reflect on the importance of symbolism. Together, discover the Catholic Christian meaning behind some symbols used in church.

Symbols point the way to a place or a person. Symbols remind us of special people, places, or things.

Symbols are all around us in church. Some of these symbols you already know. More symbols are on this page. Can you name them? Then finish each sentence.

Holy water reminds us of our
_____ .

The Eucharist is a very special meal that
_____ shares with us.

A Bible reminds us of one way
_____ speaks to us.

A lighted candle reminds us that God is with us when we _____ .

Look for these symbols the next time you go to church!

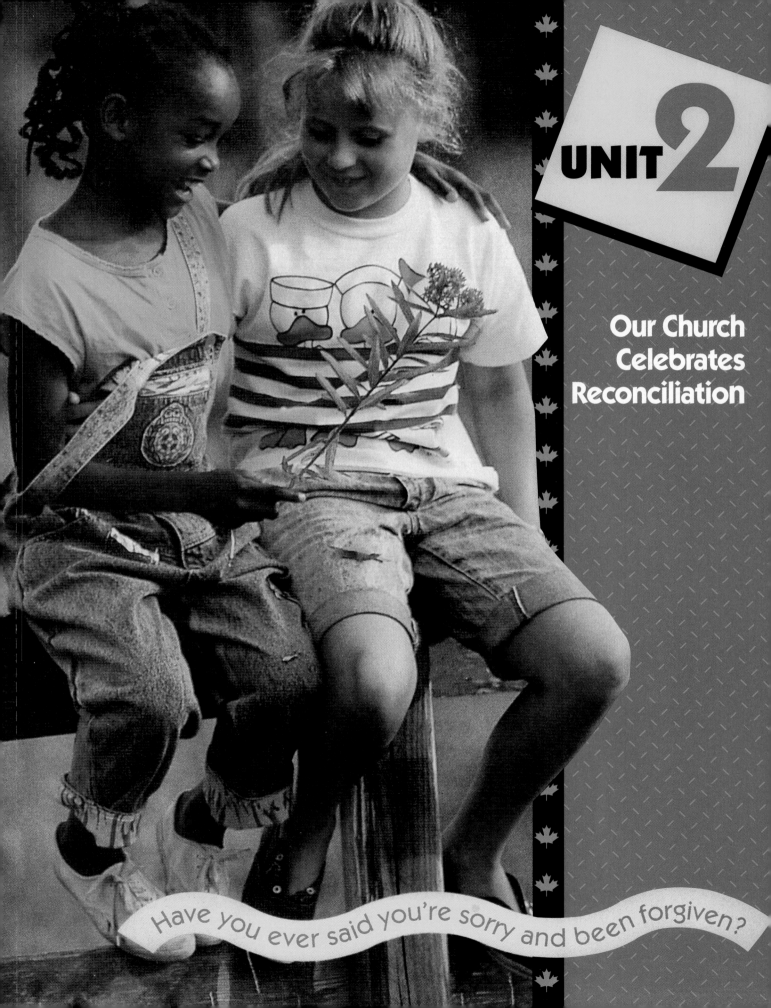

UNIT 2

Our Church Celebrates Reconciliation

Have you ever said you're sorry and been forgiven?

5

We Have a Responsibility to Care

We Need One Another

In a community everyone has needs. And everyone is needed in some way.

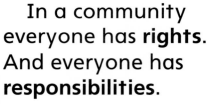

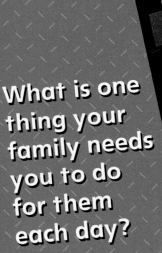

What is one thing your family needs you to do for them each day?

In a community everyone has **rights**. And everyone has **responsibilities**.

In a community everyone and everything needs care. And everyone needs to be caring.

To be family and friends in a community means to care.

We Care for Others

Jesus teaches us that we must care for others. He asks us to help others when they are in need. Jesus wants his friends to become a community of people who care.

Activity

Draw a circle around the people who are showing care.

We Believe

God calls us to be responsible and caring for others, especially people in need. We are also called to care for the earth.

New Words

right	something we deserve to have as human beings
responsibility	something we are supposed to do as members of a community

A Woman's Generous Gift

One day, Jesus and his friends went to the Temple in Jerusalem to pray. They saw many people putting money in the collection boxes for those in need.

Rich people dressed in beautiful clothes put in gold coins. Other people dressed in working clothes put in silver coins.

Then another woman walked by. She was dressed in old clothes. The woman put two pennies in the box.

Jesus and his friends watched the woman. Jesus said to his friends, "Look at the woman who has little money. She put in more than all the rest."

"What do you mean?" his friends asked. "She put in just two pennies. The others put in gold and silver."

"But they gave just a little bit of what they had," Jesus said. "The last woman gave everything she had."

Based on Mark 12:41–44

Activity

Draw or find a picture of someone who is responsible and shares with others in need.

A Saint Who Cared

Narrator: A long time ago, a woman named Elizabeth married a king named Ludwig. They lived in a country called Hungary.

Ludwig: I am happy we built a hospital to care for sick people. The hungry people are grateful when we give them baskets of food.

Narrator: Soon King Ludwig had to go to war. While he was away, he became very sick.

Messenger: My Queen, I'm so sad to tell you that your husband has died.

Elizabeth: What terrible news. My heart is broken. Let us pray for King Ludwig and for all the soldiers who have died.

Narrator: In her sadness, Elizabeth continued to care for her family, as well as for those who were poor or sick.

Enemy #1: Elizabeth gives too much money to the poor. She is spending all the money of the kingdom.

Enemy #2: We must send her away from the castle and take over the king's treasury.

Narrator: Elizabeth and her four children were forced to leave the castle.

Elizabeth: Do not worry, children. God will take care of us. We will continue to care for the sick. Somehow we will fill these baskets with food for the poor.

Narrator: Elizabeth spent the rest of her life caring for those who were sick or hungry. She is a saint who really cared for others.

Activity

Choose a word to complete each sentence. Put a check (✔)by the things that you will try to do.

smile	pray
help	share

for others.

at someone.

at home.

food or toys.

Friends of Jesus

As friends and followers of Jesus, we have a responsibility to be generous, thoughtful, and caring. Jesus teaches us how to give to others. Sometimes we are willing to share what we don't need or want. Jesus asks us to be willing to share everything, even the things we have saved just for ourselves.

As Jesus' followers, we are asked to be thoughtful. Jesus encourages us to think of other people and their needs. We try to see the needs of others before someone has to ask for our help.

Jesus wants us to care about others who feel hurt. When we have a caring heart, we include other people in our circle of friends.

Activity

Complete the poem by using the words in the box. Then read the poem alone or with others.

> done   sad
> glad   me
> none
> Responsibility

I Can Care

I'll share some of my money

With someone who has __ __ __ __ .

I've always time for helping

Get another's work all __ __ __ __ .

And when I'm full of laughing,

I'll look for someone __ __ __ .

And share with them my laughter

Until they're feeling __ __ __ __ .

I like to care for others

As others care for __ __ .

There is a word for all of this—

__ __ __ __ __ __ __ __ __ __ __ __ __ __ .

Praying to Become a Caring Community

Teacher: This is a reading from the Bible about how we should care about one another.

Followers of Jesus, let us show love in our actions and not only talk about it. Let us love one another because love is from God. Everyone who loves is a child of God and knows God, for God is love.

Based on 1 John 4:7–8

Reader 1: When someone needs help,

All: Jesus, help us care for others.

Reader 2: When someone is hurt and sad,

All: Jesus, help us care for others.

Reader 3: When someone is lonely,

All: Jesus, help us care for others.

Reader 4: When someone is sick,

All: Jesus, help us care for others.

Reader 5: When someone is poor and hungry,

All: Jesus, help us care for others.

Each Child: Here is my gift of

_____

- - - - - - - - - - - - - - - - - - - -

_____

Chapter Review

In the speech balloon, write words that say how you, as a friend of Jesus, can help. Then color the cartoon.

1. What are two things everyone in a community has?

_____
- -
_____
- -
_____

2. What is one word that describes the woman in the gospel story who gave everything she had?

_____
- -
_____

3. Talk about what we can do to show we care for people and the earth.

Jesus says, "People will know you are my friends by your love for one another."
Based on John 13:35

We Have Choices to Make

Making Choices

Life is full of choices. We make choices every day. Some choices are easy to make. Others are more difficult.

Activity

Read the stories and answer the questions.

1. Luke's father gives him a whole pack of gum. Later, his sister Anne asks Luke if he has any gum. Luke thinks to himself, "Anne doesn't know Dad gave me that gum." If you were Luke, what would you choose to tell Anne?

_____

_____

2. John didn't do his homework. He sees Kim's homework on the table. Everyone else is busy playing. John could do his homework now, or he could copy Kim's work. What would you choose to do if you were John?

_____

_____

What was the hardest choice you ever made?

3. Sarah and Jason see a wallet laying beside the path. Sarah thinks they should keep it and the money inside. Jason thinks they should try to find the owner. What would you choose to do?

_____

_____

_____

_____

Free to Choose

God gives us the freedom to choose. We can choose to do what is helpful and good for ourselves and others, or we can choose to do what hurts ourselves and others.

Jesus teaches us to choose what is helpful and loving. When we do something we know is wrong or hurt someone on purpose, we **sin**. When we don't do something we know we should do, we might also sin.

We Believe

God gives us the freedom to make choices. When we choose to do what we know is wrong, or when we choose to hurt someone on purpose, we sin.

New Word

sin Sin means to hurt someone on purpose or to do something we know is wrong. When we don't do something we know we should do, we might also sin.

The King and the Servant

There was once a servant who owed a king a lot of money. One day the king said to the servant, "You must pay back the money you owe me."

"Please give me a little more time," the servant begged.

The king felt sorry for the servant. So he said, "That's all right. I forgive your debt. There's no need to pay me or to worry anymore."

The servant was so relieved! But as he was walking home, he met a man he knew. This man owed him a dollar. The servant said, "Pay back the money you owe me, now."

"Please give me a little more time," the man begged.

The servant got very angry and grabbed the man. "I want my money now!" he shouted.

"Please," said the man. "I don't have it right now." But the servant didn't care, and he put the man in jail until he paid back the dollar.

When the king heard what his servant had done, he punished him for his selfishness and lack of care.

Based on Matthew 18:23–30

Activity

Help the children in the stories below choose to care and forgive.

Sammy took Tong's favorite baseball cards. Sammy lost them at the park. When he told Tong what happened, Tong said,
" _____ "

_____

_____ .

Ashley called Sammy a big bully and hurt Sammy's feelings. Later, Sammy told Ashley,
" _____ "

_____

_____ .

Choices to Make

Jesus gives us the Holy Spirit to help us make choices. With the Holy Spirit's help, we can choose to care for other people. The Holy Spirit can help us decide how to act in the most loving way. We can then choose the best way to help others rather than hurt them. We can choose to be kind rather than to be mean.

What's Best for Me

The choice I make
Might not always be
The one that you
Expect of me.

But sometimes I
Will choose to do
The good things that
You want me to.

Help me, Jesus,
to be free
To mostly choose
What's best for me.

Activity

Look at the pictures and read the sentences. Complete the missing words. Then circle the pictures that show someone choosing to care.

1. Greg chooses to

st_____ .

2. Nancy chooses to

sh_____ .

3. Tony chooses to

f_____ .

4. Joan chooses to

o_____ .

5. José chooses to

p_____ .

Which Is It?

It is important to know the difference between something that might be a sin and something that is only an accident. When we have an accident, it is not our fault. We don't have accidents on purpose. Accidents are things that just happen to us. Even if we break something that costs a lot of money, it is not a sin. It is an accident because we didn't do it on purpose.

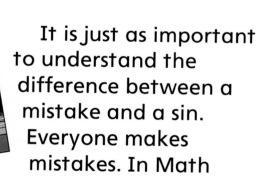

It is just as important to understand the difference between a mistake and a sin. Everyone makes mistakes. In Math class, we might make mistakes when we add or subtract. At home, we might give the dog some cat food instead of dog food. We didn't do it on purpose. We made a mistake. Making mistakes is okay. Only when we do something wrong on purpose can we call it a sin.

Activity

Now try these examples. Write **A** for accident, **M** for mistake, or **S** for sin.

You wanted to give everyone in your class an invitation to your birthday party. You forgot to give the invitations to three classmates.

_____

- - - - - - - - - - - -

_____

You scribbled all over your brother's homework paper because you thought it was scrap paper.

_____

- - - - - - - - - -

_____

You wanted to watch your favorite TV show. Your older sister changed the channel. You hit her.

_____

- - - - - - - - -

_____

Your teacher is sick and is not in school today. You decide to misbehave for the substitute teacher. You make the day very difficult for him.

_____

- - - - - - - - -

_____

Praying the Jesus Prayer

Teacher: We follow Jesus by making good choices, by listening to Jesus in prayer, and by treating one another with respect and care. One way we can listen to Jesus in prayer is by praying the Jesus Prayer:

Jesus, Son of God, have mercy on me.

Teacher: When I am hurting or sad,
All: Jesus, Son of God, have mercy on me.

Teacher: When I have hard choices to make,
All: Jesus, Son of God, have mercy on me.

Teacher: When I feel lonely or lost,
All: Jesus, Son of God, have mercy on me.

Teacher: When others ask me to forgive them,
All: Jesus, Son of God, have mercy on me.

Teacher: When I'm not sure what to do,
All: Jesus, Son of God, have mercy on me.

Chapter Review

Write **yes** next to the sentences that are choices to care about God and others. Write **no** next to the sentences that are choices to act selfishly.

_____ I forgive you.

_____ I will pray for you.

_____ I hate you.

_____ Be my friend.

_____ I'm sorry.

1. What special freedom does God give each of us?

_____

_____

2. What happens when we selfishly choose not to care?

_____

3. Talk about some things that we can do when we have to make a choice between caring or not caring.

God says,
"Choose a life of love."
Based on Deuteronomy 30:19

7

Tell a story about a time when you hurt someone or they hurt you. What did you do to make up?

We Are Called to Reconciliation

Forgiving Friends

Sometimes we say or do things that hurt someone. We may be feeling angry, or we may be acting selfishly.

Look at the pictures.
Who is feeling angry?
Who is feeling hurt?

Who cares? I don't want to see it.

Hi, Kelly! Look what I found.

Activity

Circle the picture that shows Kelly trying to be friends again.

Forgiving Friends

Friends say, "I forgive you" and "I'm sorry." Our words can help others or hurt others. Kelly's words hurt her friend's feelings. Only when she said, "I'm sorry" were they able to make up and become friends again. Kelly's friend showed that he forgave her when he said, "I forgive you."

Making up and becoming friends again is called **reconciliation**.

We Believe

God always loves us, even when we hurt others and do wrong. God will always forgive us when we are sorry. God wants us always to be willing to forgive others, too.

New Word

reconciliation   making up and becoming friends again

A Story About Reconciliation ⁓

There was a man who had two sons. One day the younger son said to his father, "I want to leave home and start a new life in the city. Give me the money that is mine so I can go."

The father was sad. His son had a good life at home and there was work for him to do. But the father did as his son asked.

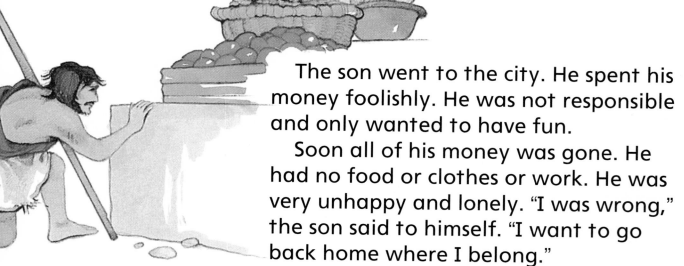

The son went to the city. He spent his money foolishly. He was not responsible and only wanted to have fun.

Soon all of his money was gone. He had no food or clothes or work. He was very unhappy and lonely. "I was wrong," the son said to himself. "I want to go back home where I belong."

At home the father worried about his son. He watched for him every day. When he saw his son walking up the road, the father ran to meet him.

"I'm sorry for what I've done," the son said. "I know I did wrong. I want to take my place at home again."

The father hugged and kissed his son. "It's all right," the father said. "I forgive you. The important thing is that you've come back to the family. How happy I am to see you."

Based on Luke 15:11–24

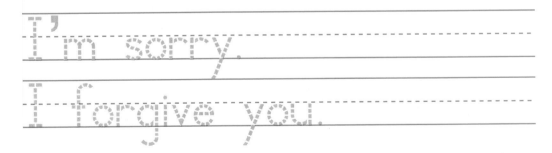

Activity

1. In this story, find the word **home**. Circle it each time you find it.

2. Now find the words of sorrow that the son said. Draw a line under them.

3. Find the words of forgiveness that the father said. Draw two lines under them.

4. Trace over the words below.

I'm sorry.

I forgive you.

Nathan, the Magnificent!

All the kids said Nathan was the best player on the school soccer team. His teammates called him Nathan, the Magnificent! But Nathan's friend, Tony, felt angry and jealous inside because he wasn't as good a player as Nathan. Sometimes Tony had to sit on the bench the whole game without ever getting to play.

Somehow Nathan knew how sad Tony felt. He could tell by the way Tony looked on those days when he had to sit out the whole game. After all, Tony was his best friend.

It took a lot of the fun out of soccer, knowing that Tony was feeling left out. But Nathan didn't know what he could do about it.

Then one day, Nathan had an idea. He asked Tony to practice with him after school without any of the other kids. The two friends passed and headed and kicked the soccer ball. Nathan and Tony had a great time! Whenever they could, the two boys practiced together.

Tony began to feel less angry. He was glad he had a friend like Nathan.

Discovering God's Grace

We know that the Holy Spirit helps us say we're sorry whenever we've hurt someone. God also gives us a wonderful gift called **grace** to help us. Grace is God's loving presence in our lives.

God's grace helps us to become friends again. Grace makes us strong so that we can make good choices. The grace of God helps us say we're sorry. Grace helps us know how others are feeling.

Activity

1. Read again the story, "Nathan, the Magnificent!" on page 86.

2. Draw one line under the sentence in the story that tells how God's grace helped Nathan know that Tony was feeling angry.

3. Circle the sentence that tells how the grace of God helped Tony feel better about Nathan.

4. Draw a box around the sentence that tells what the boys did to show that they were friends again.

New Word

grace   God's loving presence in our lives

A Prayer of Sorrow

Lord God,
I trust in your goodness
and mercy.
I am sorry
for all the wrong
things I have done.
I am sorry
for all the good things
I have not done.
I want to love you with
all my heart.

Activity

Draw a picture of yourself making friends again with
someone you have hurt and who has forgiven you.

Activity

To reconcile with our friends, we put one action on top of another. Number the blocks to show the steps of reconciling. Decide which block to start with. Number it with the number **1**. Number each of the other blocks with the numbers **2**, **3**, **4**, or **5**.

We say, "I forgive you."

_____

We do something that says we're friends again.

_____

We say we're sorry.

_____

We trust that the Holy Spirit and God's grace will help us.

_____

We pray a prayer of sorrow.

_____

Praying to Come Home to Jesus

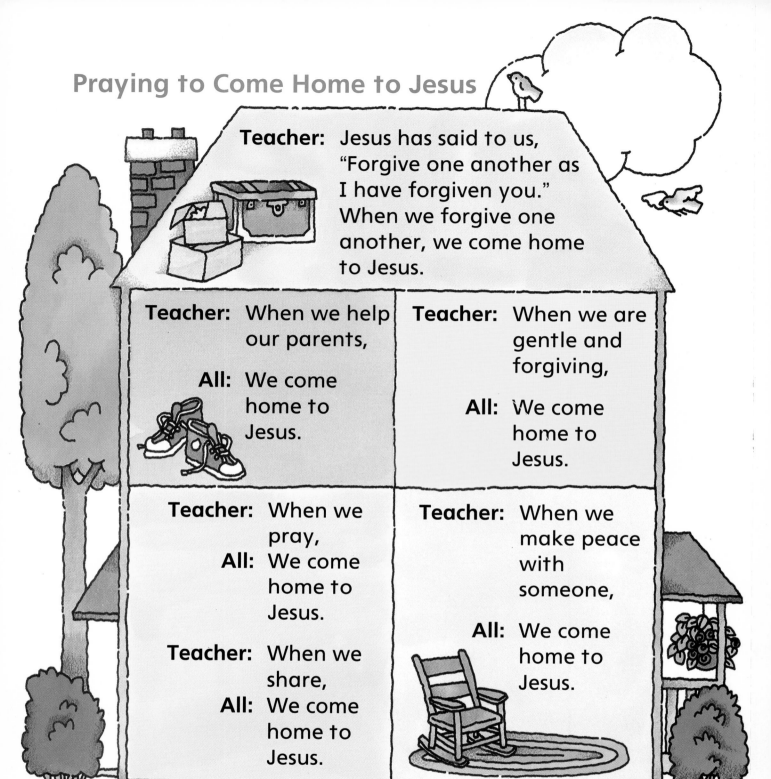

Teacher: Jesus has said to us, "Forgive one another as I have forgiven you." When we forgive one another, we come home to Jesus.

Teacher: When we help our parents,

All: We come home to Jesus.

Teacher: When we are gentle and forgiving,

All: We come home to Jesus.

Teacher: When we pray,

All: We come home to Jesus.

Teacher: When we share,

All: We come home to Jesus.

Teacher: When we make peace with someone,

All: We come home to Jesus.

Teacher: Jesus, we know that you always welcome us to your home of grace and forgiveness. It is so good to come home to you!

All: Amen.

Chapter Review

Circle the word hidden in each line.

P	F	R	I	E	N	D
H	U	R	T	B	G	W
B	K	U	G	O	D	B
F	O	R	G	I	V	E
H	M	S	O	R	R	Y

1. What does God want us to do when others hurt us?

_____

- - - - - - - - - - - - - - -

_____

2. What do we call the process of making up and being friends again?

_____

- - - - - - - - - - - - - - -

_____

3. Talk about how we can make up with someone when we have hurt them.

> **Forgive each other just as the Lord has forgiven you.**
> **Based on Colossians 3:13**

8

We Celebrate Reconciliation

How do you feel when you know that you have hurt someone on purpose?

Asking Forgiveness

To say that I am sorry
Is sometimes hard to do.
So I always try to say it
By things I do for you.

To make up isn't easy.
It takes a lot of strength
  inside.
But after I have done it,
I'm always glad I tried.

Jesus Teaches Us to Forgive

Jesus teaches us about forgiveness. This story about forgiveness is found in the Bible.

A friend of Jesus, whose name was Peter, came to Jesus and asked, "Lord, when someone hurts me, how often must I forgive? Is seven times enough?" "No," said Jesus, "not seven times, but seventy times seven times."

Based on Matthew 18:21–22

The Sacrament of Reconciliation

Catholics have a special way of showing sorrow and asking God's forgiveness. We call it the **sacrament of Reconciliation**. In this sacrament we tell God we are sorry for our sins. In this sacrament the priest brings us God's forgiveness.

ctivity

Underline the name of the sacrament in which we show sorrow for our sins and ask God's forgiveness.

New Word

sacrament of Reconciliation the sacrament in which we say we are sorry for our sins and celebrate God's forgiveness

Thinking About Our Choices

It is good to ask ourselves questions about the choices we make every day. We can think about how we have chosen to hurt others, ourselves, and the earth on purpose. We call this an examination of conscience. Examining our consciences helps us grow into more caring and loving persons. It is something Catholics do carefully before they celebrate the sacrament of Reconciliation.

An Examination of Conscience

Use these questions to help you think about your everyday words and actions.

Caring for God

- Do I listen and talk with God?
- Do I thank God for making me special?
- Do I thank God for all my gifts and talents?
- Do I tell God I'm sorry when I am selfish and don't share my gifts and talents with others?

Caring for Myself

- Do I take care of my health?
- Do I try to learn new things from my family, my teachers, and my friends and neighbors?

Caring for Others

- Do I tell the truth?
- Am I kind to other people, especially to people who are different from me?
- Do I help others?
- Do I listen to others?
- Do I forgive people who hurt me?
- Do I obey my parents and others who care for me?
- Do I thank other people for what they do for me?

Caring for Things

- Do I take care of what I have?
- Do I share my things?
- Do I respect what belongs to others?
- Do I treat animals and the earth with care?

Activity

Draw yourself making a good choice.

José Asks Questions

"Why do Catholics celebrate the sacrament of Reconciliation?" José asked his mother.

"Because, José," Mrs. Riós said, "the Church gives us this very special way of saying that we're sorry for our sins. The sacrament of Reconciliation also gives us God's forgiveness and peace."

José thought about that for a moment. Then he asked, "What happens when you go into that little room?"

"Well, we call that room the reconciliation room. When we go in, the priest welcomes us. Then we read together from the Bible," answered Mrs. Riós.

"When do you **confess** your sins?" asked José.

"That comes next. I tell the priest how I may have hurt myself or others on purpose. Then the priest gives me a **penance**. A penance is something we do that shows that we are really sorry for being selfish and unloving," answered Mrs. Ríos.

José had another question. "How does God know that you are sorry for your sins?"

"God knows I'm sorry because next I say a prayer of **contrition**. Contrition means to be sorry. I also promise to try not to sin again."

"Then you go home, right, Mom?" José asked.

"Not yet, José," said Mrs. Ríos. "Before I leave the reconciliation room, the priest gives me **absolution**. He forgives me and blesses me in Jesus' name and in the name of the Christian community. I can now leave in peace."

José's mother smiled at him. José could sure ask a lot of questions!

New Words

confess	telling our sins to a priest in the sacrament of Reconciliation
penance	A penance is a prayer or good action the priest asks of us. Doing a penance shows God that we are sorry and want to be more caring.
contrition	to be sorry
absolution	the words of forgiveness the priest prays over us in the sacrament of Reconciliation

We Believe

In the sacrament of Reconciliation, we tell God we are sorry. We ask God to forgive us for our sins. We promise to try not to sin again. God forgives us through Jesus Christ and the Church.

Now that you better understand what takes place in the sacrament of Reconciliation, follow Samantha as she celebrates the sacrament with Father Connor.

Samantha Celebrates the Sacrament of Reconciliation

Before Samantha goes into the reconciliation room, she thinks about how much God loves her. She knows God will forgive her sins. Sam thinks about how she chose to hurt her friendship with God, others, herself, and the earth. She thinks about times when she ignored her responsibilities. Sam knows some of her choices were wrong.

◀ **1.** Now Sam is ready to go to the reconciliation room. Father Connor welcomes her.

◄ **2.** Father Connor and Samantha read together from the Bible. They read about how good God is and how God is always ready to forgive.

▼ **3.** Samantha confesses her sins. She tells Father Connor that she has done things she knows were wrong and has hurt other people on purpose.

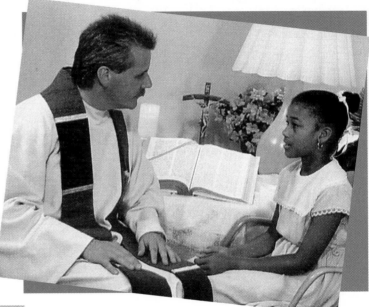

► **4.** Father Connor talks to Sam for a few minutes. He helps her find ways to love others as Jesus wants us to love them. Then Father Connor gives Samantha a penance. He asks Sam to say a prayer or to do a kind act to show her love for others and sorrow for her sins.

▲ **5.** Sam tells God that she is sorry and that she will try not to sin again. She asks forgiveness. She says a prayer of contrition.

◄ **6.** Father Connor gives Samantha absolution. He forgives and blesses her in Jesus' name and in the name of the Christian community. Father Connor then offers Sam a sign of peace. She can leave in peace.

Praying for Forgiveness

Teacher: When we hurt others,
    All: We live in darkness.

Teacher: When we don't share,
    All: We live in darkness.

Teacher: When we cause trouble
    in school,
    All: We live in darkness.

Teacher: When we don't pray,
    All: We live in darkness.

Teacher: When we care for others,
    All: Jesus' light shines.

Teacher: When we share our things,
    All: Jesus' light shines.

Teacher: When we cooperate
    at school,
    All: Jesus' light shines.

Teacher: When we pray,
    All: Jesus' light shines.

Teacher: We are forgiven.
    We are at peace.
    Let us live this day
    in the light of Jesus.
    All: Amen.

Chapter Review

Draw a line to match the words with their meanings.

confess your sins

a penance

an examination of conscience

absolution

a prayer of sorrow

telling the priest how you have hurt others

thinking about things you did or said that you know were wrong

a prayer or good action the priest asks of you to show God that you are sorry

a prayer that tells God you are sorry and asks forgiveness

a blessing of forgiveness

1. What is another word for sorrow?

_____

- -

_____

2. What do we ask God for in the sacrament of Reconciliation?

_____

- -

_____

3. Talk about ways we can make up with other people and with God.

Let us always ask God to forgive us.

Based on Hebrews 4:16

We all have rights and responsibilities because we are followers of Jesus. Name some of your rights and responsibilities.

_____

_____

_____

_____

_____

We make
choices every day.
Name one good
choice you can make.

_____

_____

_____

_____

Read the words in the columns. Then draw
a line from the words to the correct word box.

making up   good choices

hurt on purpose   Sin   selfish choices

I forgive you.   I'm sorry.

Reconciliation   grace

END

UNIT **2** REVIEW

Circle the correct word
to finish each sentence.

1. In a community everyone
has a _____ to care.

responsibility   need

2. In Jesus' story the poor woman gave
more than the rich people because she gave _____ .

silver and gold   all she had

3. Jesus says, "People will know you are my friends by
your _____ one another."

love for   sadness

4. When we hurt someone on purpose, we _____ .

forget   sin

5. The _____ _____ helps us
to say, "I'm sorry."

Holy Bible   Holy Spirit

Think about "A Story About Reconciliation."
Put an **X** by the true sentences.

6. _____ When we are mean and hurt someone, we can never make up with them.

7. _____ Reconciliation is the process of making up and being friends again.

8. _____ God always forgives us when we are sorry.

9. _____ In the story, the father did not forgive his younger son.

10. Number these parts of the sacrament of Reconciliation in their right order. Use the numbers **1** through **4**.

_____ receive absolution

_____ confess your sins

_____ accept a penance

_____ pray an act of sorrow

RESPONDING TO WHAT I'VE HEARD

When people talk to us, they tell us about their feelings or about things they want us to know. I can let someone know I have heard what he or she has said by saying back, or restating, the message.

Activity

Look at the pictures below. Tell if the person who is listening in each picture is restating a feeling message or an information message.

Activity

Pretend you are the person listening to what is being said. Restate the feeling message. Write your response in the box.

> I WANTED TO PLAY BALL. THE OTHER KIDS WOULD NOT LET ME JOIN THE GAME.

> YOU SOUND VERY _____
> - - - - - - - - - - - - - - - - - -
> _____ .

Now restate the information message. Write your response in the box.

> I WANTED TO PLAY BALL. THE OTHER KIDS WOULD NOT LET ME JOIN THE GAME.

> YOU REALLY WANTED TO _____
> - - - - - - - - - - - - - - - - - -
> _____ .

Following Jesus

Jesus wants us to show respect for others. Restating what has been said tells the speaker that I am listening and that I understand the message. Restating is one way to show respect.

A Prayer

Jesus, help me care about others. Help me listen. Help me hear. Help me respond in a way that says to the other person, "You are important." Amen.

OPENING DOORS

A Take-Home Magazine™

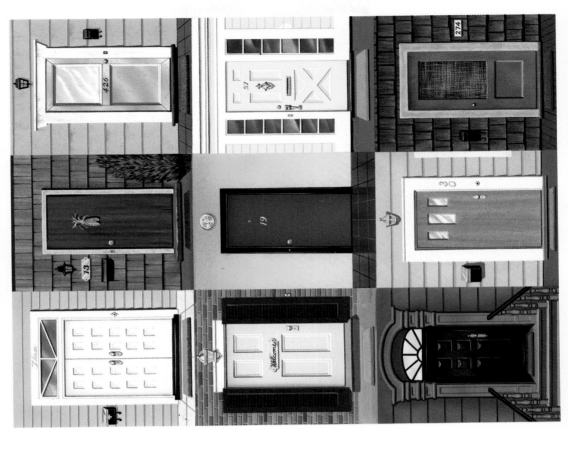

Growing Closer

Think of one thing you can do as a family that will bring a little more peace to your home. Write it on a separate sheet of paper. Post it on the refrigerator door!

Ask your family to describe what the word PEACE means to them. Record their answers on a separate sheet of paper.

Answers for pages 4-5: Lord, Christ, Lord; Lamb of God, mercy

Looking Ahead

Unit 3 will help your child understand that the people at Mass are a community gathered together in Jesus' name. Your son or daughter will also learn that the first part of the Mass, the Liturgy of the Word, is an important part of the celebration. In the Liturgy of the Word, we are reminded that our Church is the community of those who hear God's word and keep it.

MODELS OF FORGIVENESS

"Lord Jesus, you have shown us the way to the Father: Lord, have mercy."
—Roman Missal

The central message of Jesus beckons all Christians to provide for others the same unconditional forgiveness modeled in Jesus. As Christians we believe that the very life of Jesus shows us the limitless love of God the Creator and Father, the God who continuously seeks us out, even when we have turned away. When assured of this truth, we can confidently learn to trust God's goodness and seek God's mercy without fear.

Children, too, need this kind of assurance. Only when they are confident that they will be loved and forgiven—in spite of anything they have said or done—will they initiate or respond to any kind of peacemaking effort. This confidence comes first and foremost from a nurturing relationship at home.

According to the revised rite, there are different ways to celebrate the sacrament of Reconciliation.

- *anonymously* (behind a screen)
- *face to face* (sitting next to or across from the priest)
- *during a communal Reconciliation service* (celebrated with other members of the parish, with the opportunity for private confession)

Each of these ways of celebrating the sacrament has the following common elements:

- *a Scripture reading telling of God's mercy*
- *a confession of sins*
- *a discussion of ways to improve*
- *an act of contrition*
- *absolution given by the priest in the name of Jesus and the Catholic Christian community*
- *a penance as a sign of the person's desire to change for the better*

If it's been a while since you celebrated this sacrament, now may be a good time to try again. Chances are, you'll be pleasantly surprised!

Parents are often the image of God for their children. Just as the first disciples knew the Father through Jesus, our children come to know God through us. By experiencing a loving and forgiving relationship with their parents or guardians, children can begin to believe in a loving and forgiving God. Gradually, then, our children will freely join us in praying "Lord, have mercy," trusting that a compassionate God loves them and invites them to come closer to Jesus, our Reconciler, both in the eucharistic celebration and in all the grace-filled moments of their lives.

The Sacrament of Reconciliation

Many Catholic children celebrate the sacrament of Reconciliation sometime during the second grade year. If your son or daughter is preparing for first Reconciliation you may find yourself examining the value of this sacrament and what it really means.

The sacrament of Reconciliation may have been called *Confession* or *Penance* when you were a child. You may still hear the sacrament referred to by those titles. The emphasis in years gone by, however, was on confessing the sins you had committed and doing penance. On December 4, 1963 the bishops of the Second Vatican Council issued the "Constitution on the Sacred Liturgy," calling for a revised rite of Penance that "more clearly expressed the nature and effects of this sacrament." Instead of emphasizing sin, the revised rite would emphasize the real meaning of the sacrament: God's mercy and redeeming love.

To understand this shift in emphasis, consider Jesus' parable of the Prodigal Son. In the story, the son demands his inheritance, then leaves home and squanders it on immoral living. The point of the story, however, is not the son and how sinful he is but rather the father's mercy and forgiveness.

Likewise, the revised *Rite of Penance* emphasizes God's forgiving love for us. No matter what sin we may have committed or how long we've been away, God always welcomes us back! Through the sacrament we are not only reconciled to God, we are also reconciled with the other members of the Christian community.

Jesus, Our Reconciler

Remind your child that Jesus came among us to tell us how much God loves us. We call Jesus our Reconciler because he brought us back to God, our loving Father. Review with your child the following Mass prayers. Help him or her fill in the missing words. Then discover with your son or daughter the meaning of the Sign of Peace.

At Mass we remember Jesus, our Reconciler. We remember God's love and forgiveness. We pray these prayers.

_____, _____ have mercy.

_____, have mercy.

_____, have mercy.

_____, you take away the sins of the world,

have _____ on us.

Jesus asks us to make peace with everyone. We show that we forgive one another when we share a sign of peace at Mass. We show that we care for one another when we say, "Peace be with you."

Check the ways your family shares a sign of peace with others at Mass.

____ Shaking hands   ____ Saying "Peace be with you"

____ Hugging   ____ Waving at others

____ Giving a family member a kiss   ____ _____

Pray these prayers the next time you go to Mass. Greet everyone around you with a sign of peace.

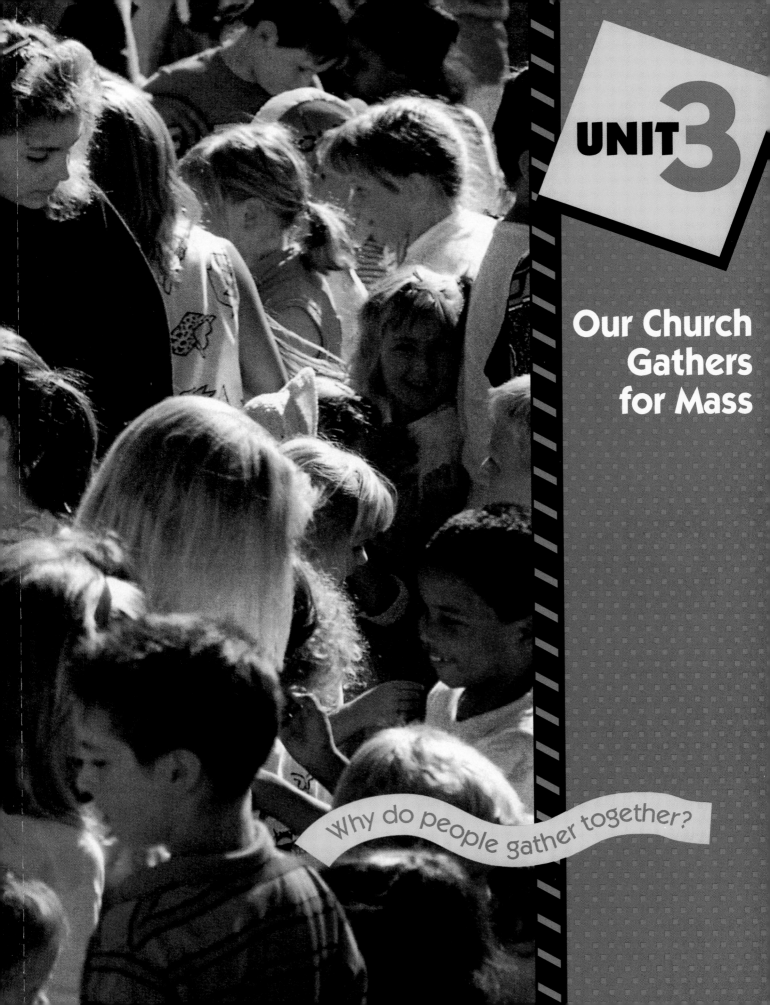

UNIT 3

Our Church Gathers for Mass

Why do people gather together?

We Gather Together for Mass

Activity

These are pictures of Sunday gatherings of people. What have they come together to do?

▲ Mass at San Jose Mission, San Antonio, Texas

▲ Mass at San Jose Parish, Austin, Texas

▲ Mass at a Canadian Eskimo village

People often gather to do things together. What are your favorite gathering times?

Friends of Jesus Gather

Jesus loved his friends. People felt special when they were with Jesus. He really listened to them.

Jesus' friends also loved to listen to his stories. They often gathered around him at mealtimes and other times to hear his wonderful stories and teachings.

We come together as friends and disciples of Jesus when we gather at **Mass**. At Mass we pray together and listen to Jesus' stories and other readings from the Bible. We also share a special meal with Jesus.

Activity

Who gathers with you for Mass? Write their names here.

_____

- -

_____

- -

_____

- -

_____

We Believe

The Catholic community gathers to celebrate a special meal with Jesus. We come together as friends and disciples of Jesus when we gather at Mass.

New Word

Mass The Mass is a special meal with Jesus. At Mass we pray together and listen to God's word from the Bible.

People liked to gather around Jesus. These gospel stories tell about some of those times.

Jesus Welcomes a Child

One day Jesus' disciples and many other people were gathered around him, listening to Jesus' teachings and stories.

The disciples asked him, "Jesus, who is the greatest in the kingdom of heaven?"

Jesus called a little child over and said, "Look at this child. Unless you change your hearts and become like little children, you will not have a place in my Father's kingdom."

Everyone was surprised by Jesus' answer. Then Jesus said, "Anyone who welcomes a little child such as this one, also welcomes me."

Based on Matthew 18:1-5

A Man Named Nicodemus

Another time, a man named Nicodemus came to Jesus at dinner time. He had heard that Jesus was a good teacher and Nicodemus wanted to talk with him.

"Teacher," Nicodemus said. "We know that you are a teacher who has come from God. No one can do such wonderful things unless God is with him."

Based on John 3:1-2

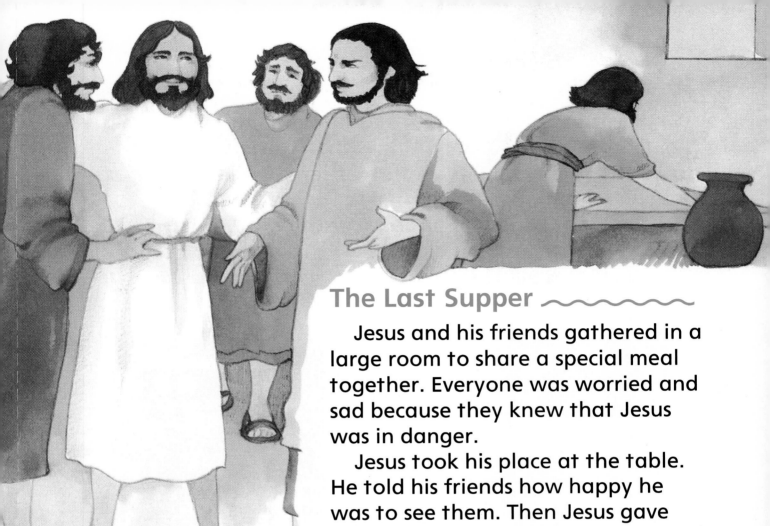

The Last Supper

Jesus and his friends gathered in a large room to share a special meal together. Everyone was worried and sad because they knew that Jesus was in danger.

Jesus took his place at the table. He told his friends how happy he was to see them. Then Jesus gave thanks to God for his friends and for the food they were about to eat.

Based on Matthew 26:26-27

Activity

Draw a picture of Jesus telling a story to friends who have gathered around him. Put yourself in the picture.

Greeting Those Who Gather

It was the Flanagan family's turn to greet and welcome the people to the 9 o'clock Mass. When the Flanagans arrived at Saint Paul Church, Father Jerry greeted them. Then he put on his green vestments. Before long, John, Michelle, and Diana, the altar servers for the Mass arrived. They lighted the candles on the altar. Then they placed the gifts that would be used during Mass on a small table near the entrance of the church.

"The Riós family is bringing up the gifts today," Mr. Scanlon, the usher, told Father Jerry. Soon it was time to greet the people who were coming to Mass. Erin and her family smiled and said, "Good morning!" to everyone.

When it was nine o'clock, the ministers lined up. John carried the cross and led the **procession**. The other altar servers followed. Mrs. Santini carried God's word in the lectionary high so that everyone could see it. Then came Father Jerry.

As the procession started down the aisle, all the people stood to sing and praise God.

Activity

Draw a picture that shows what the Sunday gathering looks like at the church where you go to Mass.

New Word

procession   people walking in line for a special reason

Welcoming a Guest

Mr. Dawson was bringing home a special dinner guest. Everyone in the family was reminded to be friendly and polite.

"When Mr. Parker gets here," Mrs. Dawson said, "be sure to say hello and tell him your name."

When their dinner guest arrived, the Dawson family greeted him at the door.

Mrs. Dawson said, "It's so good to see you, Mr. Parker. Come in and sit down in the living room."

Mr. Dawson took the guest's coat and hung it up. Michael brought Mr. Parker a cold drink. Lisa showed him her new kitten. Everyone tried to make Mr. Parker feel welcome.

Activity

How does your family welcome guests? Write about it here.

The Priest Welcomes Us

When the people have gathered and the procession is finished, the priest turns to the people and greets them by saying, "The Lord be with you."

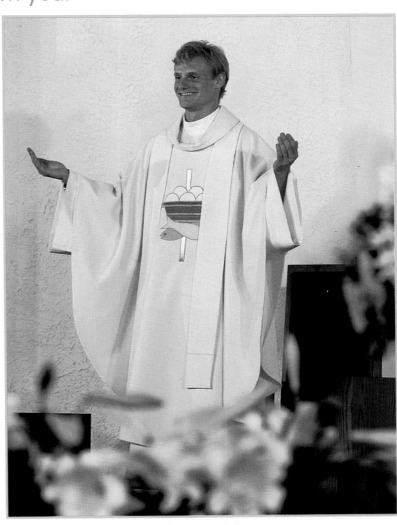

The people return the greeting with the words, "And also with you."

This greeting reminds us that Jesus is present with us in a special way as we gather at Mass.

The priest then welcomes us to the celebration of the Mass. He tells us that it is good that we have gathered together to listen to God's word and to share the gift of Eucharist.

Activity

Practice the greeting used at Mass by tracing over the letters below.

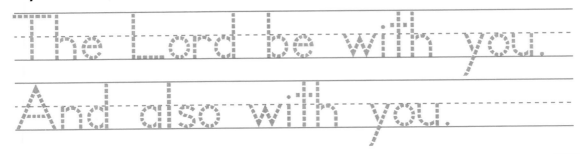

The Lord be with you.

And also with you.

Praying with a Procession

Teacher: Today we will have a procession to praise God. Let us process to the prayer table, remembering that God is here with us.

Teacher: The Lord be with you.

All: And also with you.

Teacher: O great and wonderful God, you always listen to our prayers. Let our procession today be our prayer. May it give you glory. We pray this prayer and all our prayers in the name of Jesus, your Son.

All: Amen.

Chapter Review

Choose a word to fill in each blank.

family   Jesus   friends

Thank you, God, for giving us Sundays!

On Sundays we share a special meal with

_____   _____

_____ We gather with _____ and

_____ to say thank you for sending us _____ .

Thank you, God, for giving us Sundays!

1. What do we call the special meal we share with Jesus?

_____

_____

2. Who gathers to share a special meal with Jesus?

_____

_____

_____

_____

3. Talk about ways that sharing in the Mass can help us to be kinder and more helpful in our other gatherings.

Jesus says, "Where two or three gather in my name, I am there with them."

Based on Matthew 18:20

10

We Listen to God's Word

1. Who's the best storyteller you know?

_____

- -

2. What's your favorite story?

_____

- -

3. What story do you like to listen to again and again?

_____

- -

When do you do your best listening?

Jesus was a wonderful storyteller. This is a gospel story that tells about a time when Jesus asked people to listen carefully to what he was telling them.

Jesus Teaches the People

One day, Jesus was walking along the seashore. A large crowd of people gathered to listen to him.

Jesus wanted everyone to be able to see him and hear him. He climbed into a fishing boat. He welcomed the people, sat down in the boat, and began teaching those who had gathered on the shore.

"Listen carefully," Jesus said. Then he told them many things about God. He told them how God wants them to live.

When he finished teaching, Jesus said, "Whoever has ears to hear me, listen well!"

Based on Mark 4:1-2, 9

The Bible is full of wonderful stories about God and God's people. Here is a story from the first part of the Bible.

Noah

A long time ago, there lived a man named Noah. Noah had a wife and three sons. Noah and his family were good people. They loved God very much, and God loved them.

The Lord asked Noah to build a large boat called an ark. On the ark, Noah's family and some animals would be safe from the flood waters that were to come.

It rained for forty days and forty nights. The land became flooded. Inside the ark Noah, his family, and the animals were safe.

Noah's family gave thanks to God for saving them and all the animals from the flood. A rainbow in the sky is a sign of God's promise not to flood the earth with water again.

Based on Genesis 6-9

Here is a story that Jesus told his disciples. It is from the second part of the Bible.

The Mustard Seed

The kingdom of heaven is like a mustard seed. The farmer plants a mustard seed in a field. It is the smallest seed but it grows into the largest tree of all. It becomes a tree so large that birds come and build nests in its branches.

Based on Matthew 13:31-32

ctivity

Draw a picture of your favorite Bible story.

The Liturgy of the Word

Jesus spoke God's word to the people on the seashore. We believe that Jesus speaks God's word to us, too, each time we listen to the readings at Mass. We call this part of the Mass the **Liturgy of the Word**.

The First Reading

The first reading is usually taken from the first section of the Bible, called the **Old Testament**. It tells about God and God's people who lived before Jesus was born.

The Responsorial Psalm

The next part of the Liturgy of the Word is called the **responsorial psalm**. The song leader and the parish community sing this special prayer song together.

The Second Reading

The second reading is taken from the second section of the Bible called the **New Testament**. It tells about Jesus, his disciples, and the first Christian communities. The second reading is usually a reading from one of Paul's letters to the first Christians.

Activity

Use the words on the scroll to finish part of a letter that Paul wrote to one of the first Christian communities.

Jesus

God

faith

peace

pray

Grace and _____ to you from _____ our Father, and from his Son, _____ ! I thank God every day for you because you have great

_____ in Jesus. I _____ for you each day and hope that soon I will be able to visit you.

Your friend in Jesus,
Paul
Based on Romans 1:8-10

New Words

Liturgy of the Word	The Liturgy of the Word is the first part of the Mass.
Old Testament	The Old Testament is the first section of the Bible. It tells about God and God's people who lived before Jesus.
responsorial psalm	a psalm we sing after the first reading
New Testament	The New Testament is the second section of the Bible. It tells about the life and teachings of Jesus, his disciples, and the first Christians.

We Believe

Jesus speaks God's word to us at Mass, especially during the Liturgy of the Word.

The Liturgy of the Word Continues

We have already learned about some of the Scripture readings read at Mass. Now we will read about two more important parts of the Liturgy of the Word.

The Gospel

The third reading is called the **gospel**. It is the most important reading because it tells the story of Jesus' life and teachings. Gospel stories help us know how to love and care for others. When we listen to the gospel, we stand as a sign of our love for Jesus.

The Homily

Then the priest or deacon gives a special talk that helps us understand what the gospel and the other readings mean. We call this talk the **homily**.

Activity

Share what you think the gospel stories pictured below are telling you about how to live as a follower of Jesus.

New Word

gospel   The gospel is the third reading we hear at Mass. It tells about Jesus' life and teachings.

homily   A homily is a special talk by a priest or deacon that explains the readings we listen to at Mass.

Praying God's Word

Teacher: We gather in prayer today to listen to God's word. Let us listen carefully with our ears and with our hearts.

Reader 1:   A reading from the Gospel of Matthew. Jesus said, "It is written in the Scriptures 'We do not live on bread alone, but on every word that comes from God.' "

Based on Matthew 4:4

Reader 1:   The word of God is like honey in our mouths. It is sweet and it is good for us.

Teacher: Whenever we read the Bible or listen carefully when it is read to us, we are fed with the word of God.

Chapter Review

Put an **X** next to each reason below that tells why you listen carefully. Then add one more reason why you listen well.

_____ I listen to learn new things.

_____ I listen to enjoy stories.

_____ I listen to have fun.

_____ I listen to share ideas.

_____ I listen to be a good friend.

_____ _____

1. What is the first part of the Mass called?

_____

- - - - - - - - - - - - - - - - - - -

_____

2. Which reading tells of the life and teachings of Jesus?

_____

- - - - - - - - - - - - - - - - - - -

_____

We are happy when we hear God's word and obey it.
Based on Luke 11:28

3. Talk about some things we can do to help us listen more closely to God's word at Mass.

11

We Respond to God's Word

Our Response

We talk with each other in many ways. We invite people to celebrations. We teach each other. We ask questions. We tell stories. We ask for help.

Name one time when it was easy for you to answer someone who asked you a question and one time when it was hard.

We answer or **respond** to each other in many ways, too. Sometimes we answer with words or by nodding our heads. Sometimes we smile or clap our hands. And sometimes we respond by being silent and still.

What might the people in the pictures on this page be saying to each other? How are they responding to each other?

Jesus Calls Us to Respond

Jesus responded to people in many ways. He told stories to help people understand God's love and forgiveness. His stories helped people believe in him and change their lives.

Jesus wants us to listen to him, too. We can respond to Jesus by treating others with kindness and respect. We can also respond by spending time each day talking with Jesus in prayer.

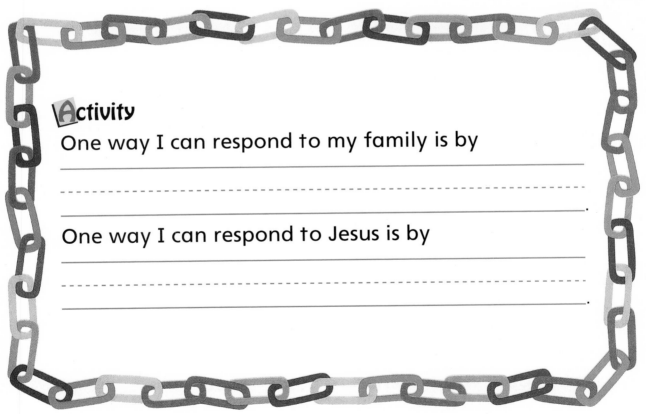

Activity

One way I can respond to my family is by

_____

- -

_____ .

One way I can respond to Jesus is by

_____

- -

_____ .

New Word

respond   to answer with words or actions

This is a story about Jesus speaking to a group of people. Discover how the people respond to him in different ways.

Jesus Talks with His Friends

Jesus had much to tell people who came to listen to him. He told them stories about God. He told them how to love and care for all people. He told them they were special. And to make them think, he asked them many questions.

Some people who listened to Jesus asked, "How can anyone believe all he says? What he says is too hard to do." So they went away.

One day Jesus asked his friends, "Do you want to leave me, too?" Everyone was silent for a minute.

Then Peter answered for them all. "Lord, to whom shall we go? Your words give us life and hope. We believe in you. We believe God sent you. We will not leave you."

Based on John 6:60-69

Activity

Choose a word from the clover leaf to fill in each blank.

Jesus, we _____ in you and want to _____ with you.

Jesus, we _____ you.

We will try to _____ your word.

Clover leaf words: stay, live, believe, love

God Sends a Messenger

One day God sent an angel as a messenger to a young woman named Mary. The angel's name was Gabriel.

"Mary," Gabriel said, "God wants you to be the mother of a special baby boy. The baby's name will be Jesus. He will be called the Son of God."

Mary wondered how she could become the mother of God's Son. Mary decided to trust God.

"Yes," Mary told Gabriel. "I will do what God wants. I will be the mother of Jesus."

Based on Luke 1:26-38

Mary Listens and Responds

Mary listened to God's call to be the mother of Jesus. At first Mary didn't understand what God was asking her to do.

Mary prayed. She decided to trust God. She listened carefully to what God was telling her. She said, "Yes, God. I will do what you ask."

ctivity

We are asked to respond to God's love for us.
Draw lines to match ways we can respond. Then
draw matching pictures.

1. God gives us parents who love and care for us.

We can respond by listening to them, obeying them, and helping them.

2. God gives us the beautiful earth and all the good things that grow on it.

We can respond by recycling aluminum cans and by using only the water we need.

3. God gives us wonderful animals.

We can respond by treating our pets and all animals with care and kindness.

4. God gives us our friends to make us happy.

We can respond by caring about them and by treating them fairly.

Responding to God at Mass

We can hear Jesus speak to us when we listen to the readings and homily during the Liturgy of the Word. We are called to respond with songs, prayers, and actions. And we are called to respond by living in a caring and responsible way.

Activity

Trace over the letters on the lines below.
Then read our responses to God's word.

The word of the Lord.

Thanks be to God.

The gospel of the Lord.

Praise to you,

Lord Jesus Christ.

At Mass we respond to God's word after each reading. We also thank Jesus for teaching us about life and about God. We praise God through songs, prayers, and actions.

Activity

Learn these gestures based on Psalm 19 as one way of responding to God's word.

The heavens tell of your glory, O God!

And all creation shouts with joy and praise.

Come, children, play on your instruments and dance.

And sing glory to our God!

We Believe

We are called to respond to God's word. At Mass we respond with words, songs, and prayers. In our lives we respond by doing what Jesus asks of us.

Praying with Faith

Teacher: We come to our prayer table with great faith in God, our Creator, and in Jesus, our Friend. Let us pray together about some things we believe as children of God.

All: We believe in you, God!

We believe that you made us in your own image and that we are like you.

We believe that you sent us Jesus, your greatest gift. And we believe that Jesus shows us who you are.

We believe in the Holy Spirit, who is your Spirit. And we believe that the Holy Spirit helps us each day to make good choices.

We believe that your love will never leave us.

We believe in you, God!

Amen.

WE BELIEVE IN YOU GOD

Holy Bible

Chapter Review

The five words hidden in the puzzle tell of ways we can respond to God in our lives. Circle each word you find.

L	T	H	A	N	K	S
F	E	O	M	I	L	U
A	P	K	F	M	O	Z
I	C	A	R	E	V	P
T	Z	P	O	L	E	D
H	G	O	T	U	C	N
T	P	R	A	I	S	E

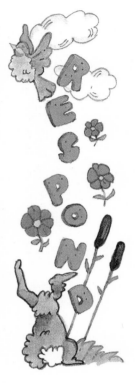

1. What word describes what we do when we answer someone with words or actions?

----

2. How can we respond to God's word at Mass?

----

3. Talk about some things we can do to respond to Jesus and his teachings.

"Lord, you have the words of life."
Based on John 6:68

We Pray for People

Many people need or want us to pray for them. What are some reasons why they ask us to pray for them?

Praying for Others

I know that someone's hungry.
I know that someone's sad.
I know that I have much more
Than many ever had.

I know that I should share my things.
I know that I should care.
And one thing I can do right now
Is help someone with prayer.

God Asks Us to Pray

God wants us to pray for the world and its people. When we pray for people, we show our love for them.

We can pray alone or with others. God says that when we pray with others, our prayer is strong. When we pray at Mass, we pray with others.

This family is praying together. When do you pray with your family? ▶

◀ This class is praying for the earth. How can your class pray for God's creation?

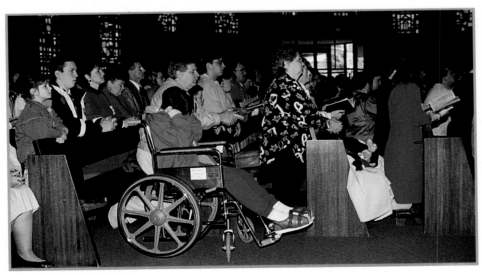

◀ This Christian community is praying for those who are sick. Whom does your Christian community pray for?

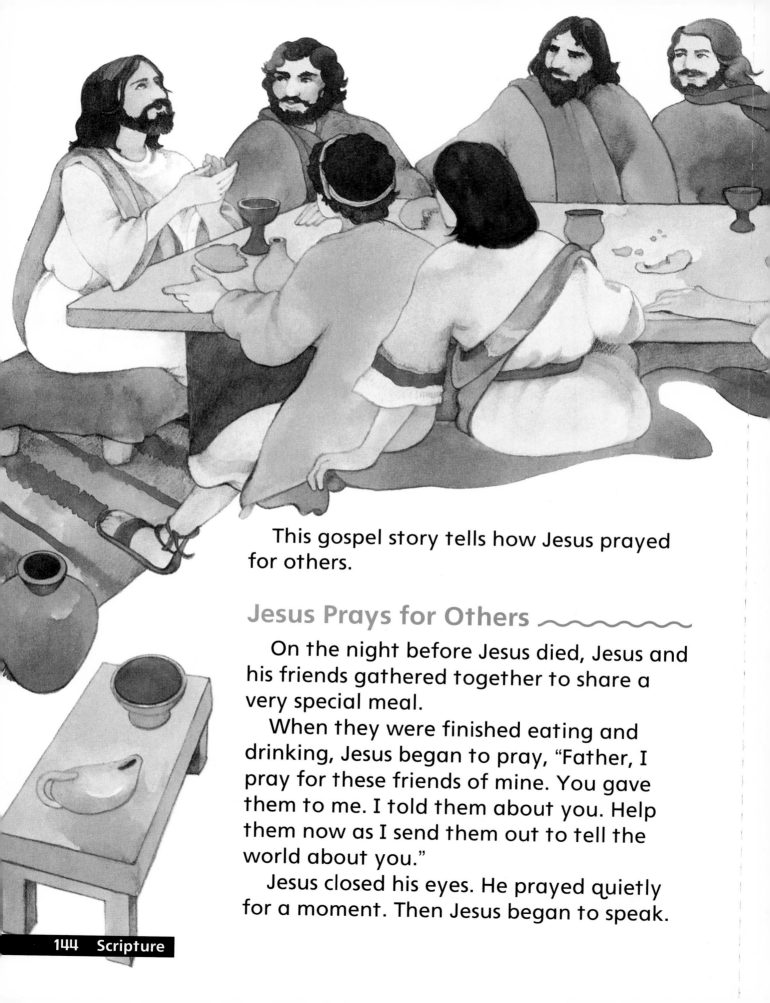

This gospel story tells how Jesus prayed for others.

Jesus Prays for Others

On the night before Jesus died, Jesus and his friends gathered together to share a very special meal.

When they were finished eating and drinking, Jesus began to pray, "Father, I pray for these friends of mine. You gave them to me. I told them about you. Help them now as I send them out to tell the world about you."

Jesus closed his eyes. He prayed quietly for a moment. Then Jesus began to speak.

"Father," Jesus said, "I do not pray just for these friends of mine. I pray for people all over the world. Help them live like brothers and sisters. Love them as you love me. Be with them as you are with me."

Based on John 17:1-26

Activity

Complete this picture of a place where Jesus might have prayed. Draw yourself and Jesus at this place.

▲ This person is leading the Prayer of the Faithful at Mass.

Praying Shows That We Care

Jesus prayed for his friends and for all people in need. Jesus prays for us, too. He wants us to show that we care by praying for one another.

We can pray for others at Mass during the **Prayer of the Faithful**. This prayer is the last part of the Liturgy of the Word. In the Prayer of the Faithful, we pray for the Church, for our country and its leaders, and for all God's people.

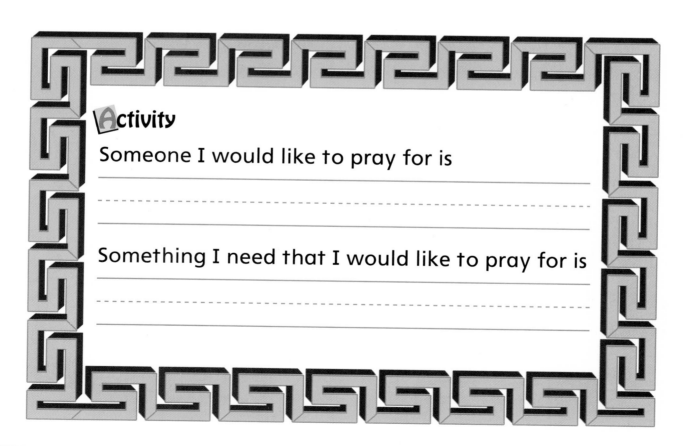

Activity

Someone I would like to pray for is

_____

_____

Something I need that I would like to pray for is

_____

_____

Prayer of the Faithful

During the Prayer of the Faithful, we can pray for people everywhere. We can pray for ourselves, too.

Leader: We pray for world leaders. Help them make good choices so that all people may live in peace.

People: Lord, hear our prayer.

Leader: We pray for those who are hungry and poor.

People: Lord, hear our prayer.

Leader: We pray for our families and friends. Help us live in peace.

People: Lord, hear our prayer.

We Believe

Jesus wants us to pray for people everywhere. We can do this any time and in many ways. At Mass we do this during the Prayer of the Faithful.

New Word

Prayer of the Faithful The Prayer of the Faithful is the last part of the Liturgy of the Word. During this prayer we pray for ourselves and for people everywhere.

Here is a story about a friend of Jesus who spends her whole life praying for God's people.

A Special Kind of Prayer

My name is Sister Anna. I am a religious sister, or nun. I live in a convent with eight other sisters. Our convent is on a farm. We have come here to live because God asked us to pray in a special way for all God's people. That's a lot of people!

Very early each morning, we get up and go into our chapel to pray. We pray for everyone who needs our prayers that day. Then we eat breakfast and begin our work.

My special job is to care for the farm animals. We have lots of cows on our farm. We also have goats, pigs, and chickens. I feed the animals and milk the cows. I make sure that the animals are clean and healthy.

Even while I work, I never stop praying. I praise God for the wonderful animals on the farm that I enjoy so much. I ask God to help parents care for their children and to heal those who are sick or hurt.

The other sisters and I eat dinner together and return to the chapel. Again we pray for people everywhere. We ask God to keep everyone safe through the night.

I like to pray as Jesus must have prayed—for everyone and at all times. I am grateful that God asked me to live as a sister of prayer.

Activity

Not everyone is asked to spend their whole lives in prayer in the same way as Sister Anna. But we are asked to pray often. Put a [✔] in front of those special times when you pray.

_____ when I get up in the morning

_____ before I eat a meal

_____ when I'm at Mass

_____ when I'm alone

_____ when I'm with others

_____ when I'm with my family

_____ before I go to bed

Praying with a Prayer Chain

There are many ways we can join our prayers together. We can pray together at Mass. We can pray with our families. We can pray with our friends and classmates.

Another way we can join our prayers together is by making prayer chains.

Make a prayer chain with your classmates or invite the other classes in your school to join you in making a school prayer chain. Follow these directions.

Step 1
Cut strips of construction paper about 11" long and 3" wide.

Step 2
On each paper strip, write the name of a person or a need that you would like to pray for. You might want to use a felt-tip marker.

Step 3
Staple or glue the strips together so that the names of the people or needs you want to pray for can be seen.

Step 4
Join your prayer chain to your classmates' chains. Hang the finished prayer chain on your classroom prayer table or in another place where it can be seen by others.

Chapter Review

Circle the word hidden in each line. Then write these words on the lines below the puzzle.

Z	M	X	F	A	T	H	E	R
P	M	I	Z	H	J	M	B	T
C	L	E	P	R	A	Y	Y	S
F	O	R	N	D	J	R	B	I
J	T	H	E	S	E	N	P	T
Q	U	F	R	I	E	N	D	S
S	U	L	O	F	L	A	Z	N
C	D	M	I	N	E	I	M	B

1. How can we help people who are in need?

2. Who taught us that we should pray for others?

3. Talk about the many ways we can pray for ourselves and for other people.

Pray always for all God's people.
Based on
Ephesians 6:18

start

Prayer of the Faithful   second reading   homily

Liturgy of the Word

gospel   responsorial psalm   first reading

finish

Unit **3** Review

Complete each sentence below by circling the correct answer. Then use these answers to fill in the puzzle.

1. The _____ tells of the life and teachings of Jesus.

      gospel   first reading

2. The _____ celebrates a special meal with Jesus.

      Reconciliation   Eucharist

3. The first part of the Mass is called the Liturgy of the

      _____ .

      Word   Altar

4. On Sunday we _____ together for Mass.

      listen   gather

5. Fill in the puzzle. Use the words you circled above.

Unit **3** Review

6. How can we respond to God's word at Mass?

_____

- -

_____

7. How can we respond to God's word in our lives?

_____

- -

_____

_____

- -

_____

Circle the correct answer.

8. We should only pray for people in need.

Yes   No

9. We can pray for people during the Prayer of the Faithful.

Yes   No

10. God wants us to pray for people everywhere.

Yes   No

11. In the story "Jesus Prays for Others," Jesus only prayed for his close friends.

Yes   No

12. The Liturgy of the Word ends with the Prayer of the Faithful.

Yes   No

EXPRESSING MY FEELINGS

Using "I" messages lets me share my feelings in a helpful way.

My feelings are an important part of me. Sharing my feelings is a good way for others to know more about me. When I feel sad, angry, or upset, others can help me feel better if I let them know how I feel. An "I" message tells how I feel and what has caused the feeling.

I feel

_____

_____ ,

when

_____

_____ .

Activity

Read the story. Write a word that tells how each child might be feeling. Then decide what "I" messages they might use.

Stacy is bothering Tim. Tim is trying to finish his work. Stacy keeps asking Tim questions.
Tim is beginning to feel

_____

_____ .

What "I" message might Tim use?
I feel

_____

_____ ,

when Stacy

_____

_____ .

Activity

Alex is at recess. Alex wants to play ball with the other kids. When Alex asks to play, the others tell him, "No, we already have our teams."

_____

Alex is feeling _____ .

What "I" message might Alex use?

_____   _____

I feel _____ when you _____ .

What should I do when I hear an "I" message?

When someone tells me how he or she feels, I need to remember to be a good listener. A good listener uses eye contact, pays attention, and remains quiet while the speaker is talking. A good listener restates the feeling or information given by the speaker.

How would you respond to Alex?

Fill in the box with what you would say to Alex.

> I FEEL LEFT OUT WHEN I DON'T GET TO PLAY.

_____

Following Jesus

Jesus always cared about people's feelings. He spent much time listening to people and speaking with them. Jesus asks us to care about other people's feelings, too. When we listen well to others, we follow Jesus.

A Prayer

Jesus, help us to be more open to telling each other how we feel. Help us to be more willing to listen to the feelings of others. Amen.

OPENING DOORS

A Take-Home Magazine™

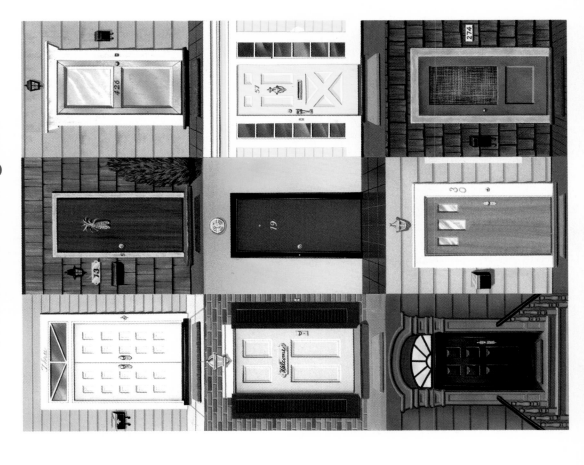

Growing Closer

EVERY FAMILY HAS stories to tell! Share some favorite family stories at mealtime or whenever the family is together. Enjoy listening to one another—if only for a few brief moments.

ASK EVERYONE in your family to listen carefully to the gospel reading the next time you go to Mass. Later at home, talk with one another about what the story might mean for your family. Encourage everyone to share their feelings about the story. Listen carefully to one another and accept everyone's ideas.

Looking Ahead

In Unit 4 your child will learn that the Eucharist is a thanksgiving celebration. At Mass we praise and thank God for many gifts, especially for the gift of God's Son, Jesus. Your son or daughter will learn that the Eucharist is a sacrificial meal. Jesus not only gave himself to us in the Eucharist but gave his life for us after much suffering.

8

A Closer Look

Responding to the Word

When those we love speak meaningful words to us, we often feel a need to respond appreciatively. God's word proclaimed at Mass can inspire in us a similar response. During the Liturgy of the Word as we listen to the story of our salvation, what more grateful replies can there be than "Thanks be to God" and "Praise to you, Lord Jesus Christ"?

Praying words of thanks and praise, then, is a natural response to the good news of our salvation. The real challenge, perhaps, lies in the way we respond to the Scriptures *with our lives.*

We are challenged each time we hear a Scripture reading to hear more than words we may have heard many times before. We are encouraged to hear the God of love speaking endearing and meaningful words to each of us, and we are challenged to find ways of responding appreciatively with our lives.

the Canticle of Mary (Luke 1:46–55); night prayer includes the Canticle of Simeon (Luke 2:29–32). In addition, the prayer contains quiet times for silent meditation.

The Liturgy of the Hours stems from our Jewish heritage. In the time of Jesus, Jews assembled each morning and evening in the synagogue to recite the Shema (shuh MAH) (Dt. 6:4–9; 11: 13–21; Numbers 15:37–41) and the eighteen blessings. Early Christians continued the practice of meeting for prayer each morning in the synagogue and for the Eucharist each evening in their homes.

If you are interested in finding out more about the Liturgy of the Hours, check with your Catholic bookstore for the revised English version, entitled *The Liturgy of the Hours According to the Roman Rite,* or ask for one of the many published versions that have been simplified for general use. You may wish to pray this prayer by yourself at home or you may choose to pray it with others at church.

The word of God always meets us where we are and beckons us to live the message in and through the particular circumstances of our daily lives. Some of us are called to respond to God's word in extraordinary ways, such as with lives of service to the poor. Most of us, however, are called to respond in more ordinary ways. Each time we forgive our spouse or child, each time we let another ahead of us in line, each time we give up an evening to help someone in need, we respond to Jesus' command to "love one another." This is good news, indeed!

Being Catholic

Christian Prayer, Morning and Evening

Prayer is an important part of Christian living. As you probably realize, there are many different ways to pray. There are memorized prayers, spontaneous prayers, individual prayers, group prayers. One kind of prayer that is growing in popularity again in some sections of our country is the Liturgy of the Hours. Many parishioners are beginning to practice this prayer, especially during the liturgical seasons of Advent and Lent.

What is the Liturgy of the Hours? Basically, it is a Scripture-based group prayer. Parts of the prayer are prayed at certain hours of the day: morning, midmorning, midday, midafternoon, evening, and night. This prayer is the official prayer of the Church for praising God and sanctifying the day. For centuries, priests and men and women religious had been required to pray the Liturgy of the Hours. But many lay people have prayed this prayer, too.

In today's Church, morning prayer (Lauds), evening prayer (Vespers), and night prayer (Compline) are the three most popular forms of the Liturgy of the Hours. The principal parts of these prayers consist of a hymn, two psalms, a brief Scripture reading, responses, intercessions, and a concluding prayer. Morning prayer includes the Canticle of Zechariah (Luke 1:68–79); evening prayer includes

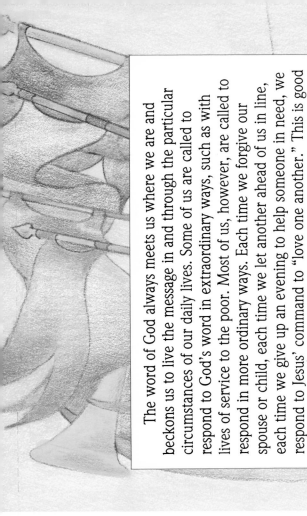

A Closer Look

Responding with Love

Read through these pages with your child. Discover together some ways of responding to the readings at Mass. Encourage your child to complete the activity. Ask others in your family to participate.

Stories are fun to hear! Sometimes we clap our hands when we hear a good story. Sometimes we just smile and feel good inside.

At Mass we listen to God's stories. We feel happy. We know God loves us.

4

We want to respond to God's stories of love. We want to thank God for loving us.

Here are some ways we can respond to God's stories of love. Try a different way each day. Then color that part of the caterpillar.

Do your homework carefully.

Be kind to your family.

Thank God for your family and friends.

Take a walk. Look for signs of God's love.

Help your family prepare dinner.

Listen carefully to your teacher.

Write a letter to someone who misses you.

Say a prayer for someone you don't like.

Clean your room without being told.

Tell your favorite Bible story to a younger brother or sister.

Listen carefully to God's stories the next time you go to Mass. Try to find some ways to respond to God's love for you.

5

UNIT 4

Our Church Celebrates the Eucharist

What's the best present you have ever received?

13

We Present Ourselves to God

We Bring Gifts

The secret of this special gift
Is like a mystery.
The love and care that it contains
Are things no one can see.

Tell about a time when you gave someone a special gift.

What are the people doing in these pictures?

Gifts to Share

There are many times when we give gifts. A special time when Catholics bring gifts to share is during the **Liturgy of the Eucharist,** the second part of the Mass. The gifts we bring to the altar are bread and wine. We also bring money and sometimes other gifts for people in need. Most of all, we bring ourselves. The Liturgy of the Eucharist begins as we prepare the altar and bring gifts for our special meal with Jesus.

Activity

Fill in the missing words.

1. We call the second part of the Mass the

_____ _____

_____ of the _____ .

2. The best gift that I can give to God

_____

is the gift of _____ .

We Believe

The second part of the Mass is called the Liturgy of the Eucharist. It begins as we prepare the altar and bring gifts for our special meal.

New Word

✦
✦
✦   **Liturgy of the Eucharist** The Liturgy of the Eucharist is the
✦   second part of the Mass. It begins as we
✦   prepare to share a special meal with Jesus.

Blessed Be God

At Mass we bring gifts of bread and wine to the altar to say thanks to God. The gifts may seem ordinary, but through them Jesus unites us with himself and with one another.

▲ The family in this picture is bringing up the gifts of bread and wine. Has your family ever brought up the gifts at Mass?

These are the gifts that ▶ the Catholic Christian community offers as thanks to God.

Then the priest holds up the paten. He asks God to bless the bread that will become Jesus, the Bread of Life. We respond, "Blessed be God forever."

Next, the priest holds up the chalice. He asks God to bless the wine that will become Jesus. Again we respond, "Blessed be God forever."

Activity

Draw the gifts we bring at Mass.

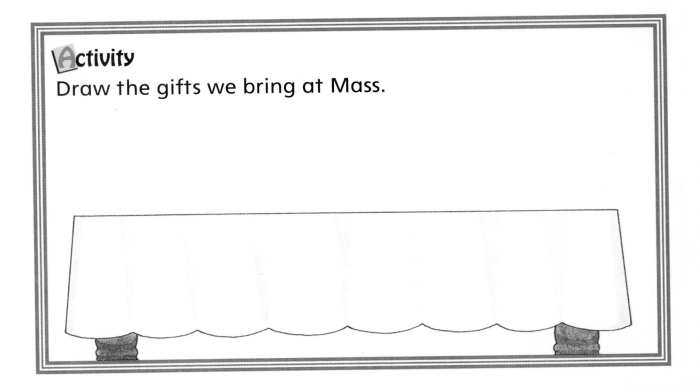

Sharing with Others

One day, Jesus and his friends wanted to go up into the mountains. Many people began to follow them. They wanted to be with Jesus and listen to him.

Jesus talked to them all day. By evening everyone was hungry. Jesus wanted to feed them. "There is a young boy here," Andrew told Jesus, "who has five loaves of bread and two fish. Although it's not much, he is willing to share them."

The boy gave his bread and fish to Jesus. Jesus thanked the boy. Jesus thanked God for the boy's gift. Then something wonderful happened. Jesus had enough food to share with all the people. There was even food left over. More than five thousand people were fed with the bread and the fish the boy had given to Jesus.

Based on John 6:1–13

Activity

Think about some of the gifts you have to share with others. Name these gifts on the pictures below.

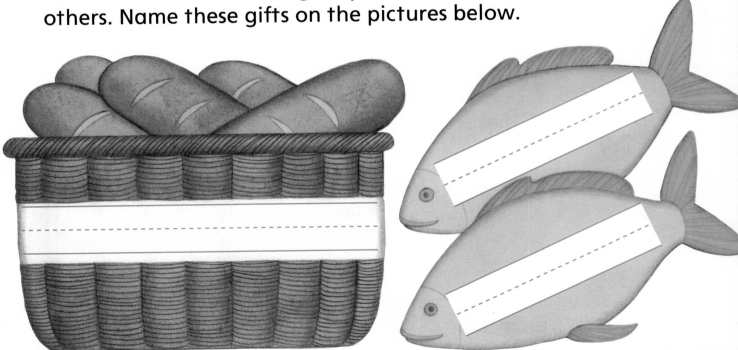

Peanut Butter Sunday

Grandpa was bending down, looking into the cupboard when Jessie arrived.

"Jessie, I need your help," he said. "Can you find the new jar of peanut butter?"

"Here it is, Grandpa!" Jessie said as she reached into the back of the cupboard.

"Thank you, Jessie. I'm taking this to church for Peanut Butter Sunday," explained Grandpa.

"On Peanut Butter Sunday, we collect peanut butter for people in our community who don't have enough money to buy groceries."

"That's a great idea, Grandpa," answered Jessie. "Here's a jar of jelly to go with it."

Grandpa smiled at Jessie. Then they both hurried off to church.

Activity

1. Circle the sentence in the story above that shows how Grandpa showed his care for those who were hungry.

2. Draw a line under the sentence that tells how Jessie showed she cared about Grandpa.

We Offer Gifts of Love

In the story, "Peanut Butter Sunday," we learn that not all gifts are gifts we buy. Some gifts come from within us.

We have many opportunities to give gifts to one another. When someone is sad, we can give the gift of our laughter. When someone needs a friend, we can give the gift of our friendship.

Activity

Finish these stories about two children who want to give the gift of themselves.

Michelle's little brother Joey didn't get to play at all in the soccer game. He said, "I never want to play soccer again!" Joey is sitting on the front steps, looking sad and disappointed. What gift could Michelle give to Joey?

_____

- - - - - - - - - - - - - - - - - - -

_____

Julio's teacher, Mrs. Sanchez, is ill and will miss school for several days. Julio really misses her. What gift could Julio give to Mrs. Sanchez?

_____

- - - - - - - - - - - - - - - - - - -

_____

Praying a Morning Offering

Teacher: Jesus, as we begin this day,

All: We offer you our hands.
Teacher: May our work and our caring give you praise.

All: We offer you our feet.
Teacher: May we play fairly and follow you.

All: We offer you our eyes.
Teacher: May we see ways we can show our love for others.

All: We offer you our ears.
Teacher: May we listen and learn well today.

All: We offer you our mouths.
Teacher: May our words be kind and gentle.

All: We offer you our whole day.
Teacher: May everything we say and do tell others that we are your friends.

All: Amen.

Chapter Review

Write a **T** if the sentence is true. Write an **F** if the sentence is false (not true).

_____ 1. There are many times when we give gifts.

_____ 2. Catholics offer gifts at Mass during the Liturgy of the Word.

_____ 3. The gifts we bring to the altar are bread and milk.

_____ 4. Most of all we bring ourselves as gifts at Mass.

_____ 5. At Mass, Jesus unites us with himself and with one another.

1. What do we call the second part of the Mass?

_____

- -

_____

2. What gifts are brought to the altar?

_____

- -

_____

Bring gifts and come to the Lord.
Based on Chronicles 16:29

3. Talk about what we can do to show thanks for all God's gifts.

We Thank God for Many Gifts

Saying Thank You

Everyone knows how important it is to say thank you. We can say it in every language and in many different ways. But no matter how we say thank you, it always means "I'm glad you did what you did!"

Activity

The children below are showing you words that mean "thank you" in different languages. Circle the picture that shows the words *thank you* in a language you can speak or would like to learn.

Remembering to say thank you is very important. Tell a story about a time when you remembered to say thank you.

Thanking God

God gives us many gifts. At Mass, we can thank God for all the gifts we have been given. A special prayer at Mass for thanking God is prayed during the **Eucharistic Prayer**.

The word <u>eucharistic</u> means "giving thanks." In the Eucharistic Prayer, the priest thanks God for our many gifts. We join the priest in a prayer of praise and thanks to God for all creation. We are especially thankful for God's greatest gift, the gift of Jesus.

Activity

What does the word <u>eucharistic</u> mean? To find out, circle every other letter. Begin with the second letter. Write the letters you circled on the lines below.

_____

- -

_____

- -

_____

New Word

Eucharistic Prayer The Eucharistic Prayer is a special prayer at Mass for praising and thanking God, especially for the greatest gift, Jesus.

We Believe

During the Eucharistic Prayer, we praise and thank God for all creation and for God's greatest gift, Jesus.

Prayers and Responses

Thanking God during the Eucharistic Prayer can help us become more thankful people in our everyday lives.

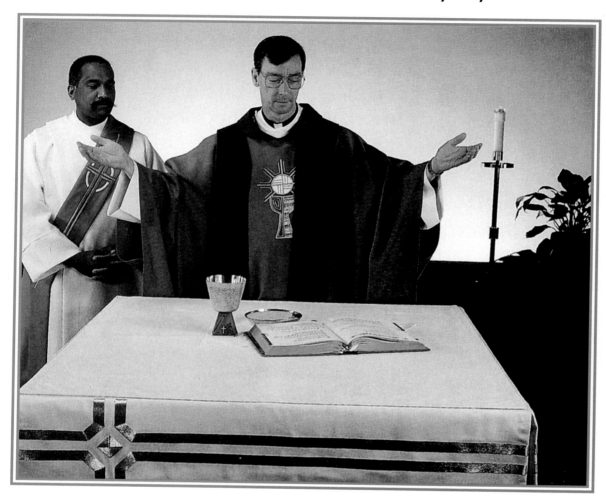

Read the prayer below. These are some of the prayers and responses that we say before the Eucharistic Prayer.

Priest: The Lord be with you.
All: And also with you.

Priest: Lift up your hearts.
All: We lift them up to the Lord.

Priest: Let us give thanks to the Lord our God.
All: It is right to give him thanks and praise.

Give Thanks Everyday

Bernard came from a large family in Wisconsin. When he grew up, he became a religious brother and later a priest. Brother Solanus, as he was called, answered the monastery door and greeted people. He thanked them for the gifts they brought. When hungry people knocked, he gave them food. Often people asked him to listen to their stories or to pray with them for healing. Brother Solanus taught people how to thank God in their daily lives.

Activity

Every day we can thank God for all the good things we have been given. Fill in the schedule below with pictures or words that show what you will thank God for at each time of day.

in the morning	
at noon	
in the afternoon	
in the evening	
at bedtime	

Only One Said Thanks

One day, Jesus was walking toward a small village. Ten men and women called out to Jesus. They stood far away from him. These people had a skin disease called leprosy.

"Jesus, help us!" they begged. Jesus felt sorry for them. He could see how sick they were. He understood how much they were hurting.

"Go up to the Temple in Jerusalem," Jesus told them. They did what Jesus said. On their way to Jerusalem, all ten of them were completely healed.

One man ran his hand over his face and arms. He felt how smooth his skin was. All the sores were gone. He praised and thanked God.

Then the man went back to find Jesus. When he saw Jesus, he ran over to him and thanked him.

Based on Luke 17:11–17

▲ What words do you think the man used to thank Jesus? What did Jesus say to him?

Activity

On the lines below, list some of the people and things you are thankful for.

One Way to Say Thanks

A long time ago in France, Pauline received a letter from her brother Pierre. Pierre worked with people in a faraway country who were very poor. He told her how the people were starving and how they had so few clothes and no money.

Pauline encouraged her friends to save a penny a week to share with those who had nothing.

"A penny of thanks for those in need is my way of saying thank you to God!" exclaimed Pauline. How do you remember to thank God?

We Give Thanks to God

During the Liturgy of the Eucharist, we gather to give thanks. Our special meal with Jesus is a time to thank and praise God for all creation. We give thanks for all God's gifts, especially for the greatest gift of all—Jesus.

At the top of the next page is a part of one of the great prayers of praise we pray during the Liturgy of the Eucharist.

Priest: Because you love us, you give us this great and beautiful world. With Jesus we sing your praise.

People: Hosanna in the highest.

Priest: Because you love us, you sent Jesus your Son to bring us to you and to gather us around him as the children of one family.

People: Hosanna in the highest.

Priest: For such great love we thank you with the angels and saints as we sing.

Priest and People: Holy, holy, holy Lord, God of power and might, heaven and earth are full of your glory.
Hosanna in the highest.
Blessed is he who comes in the name of the Lord.
Hosanna in the highest.

Activity

Color and decorate these words of praise and thanks to God who saves us.

Praying with Gestures

Teacher: We can pray with words and songs and gestures. Let us praise and thank God today by using words and gestures.

All: We bless you and thank you, God, for you are great indeed!

Teacher: You make springs in the mountains to provide water for your people.

All: We bless you and thank you, God, for you are great indeed!

Teacher: You created the birds of the sky that sing their songs from the trees.

All: We bless you and thank you, God, for you are great indeed!

Teacher: You made the moon and the sun to show us the time and the seasons.

All: We bless you and thank you, God, for you are great indeed!

Teacher: You make our hearts glad and our faces shine with joy.

All: We bless you and thank you, God, for you are great indeed!

Based on Psalm 104

Chapter Review

Talk about how these people are saying thank you.

1. Whom can we thank for all the good people and things in our lives?

_____

- - - - - - - - - - - - - - - - - -

_____

2. What prayer do we pray at Mass to praise and thank God?

_____

- - - - - - - - - - - - - - - - - -

_____

3. Talk about your favorite ways of showing thanks.

Give thanks to God for everything in the name of Jesus Christ.
Based on Ephesians 5:20

15

We Celebrate the Sacrifice of Jesus

Sharing Ourselves

Sometimes we give away things that are special to us. To give up a favorite thing is hard to do.

Felipe has a baseball glove that is very special to him. His little brother José needs a baseball glove. What do you think Felipe might do?

Tell a story about a time when you didn't want to share but you did it anyway because you loved the person.

Cathy's class is going on a special field trip. Everyone needs a partner. Cathy likes to sit with Beth, but Cathy knows that no one ever chooses Jennifer as a partner. What do you think Cathy might do?

When we give up a favorite thing out of love, we make a **sacrifice**. When we give our time and help out of love, we are also making a sacrifice.

Jesus' Love for Us

At Mass we remember how much Jesus loves us. We remember how Jesus gave his life for us on the cross. He made this sacrifice for us because he loves us.

Jesus gave his life for all his friends, including us. At Mass, we celebrate the love Jesus has for us.

Activity

Think of someone in your family who has made a sacrifice for you. What did this person sacrifice? Write it on the lines below.

_____

_____

_____

_____

_____

_____

_____

New Word

✦
✦ **sacrifice**   to give something out of love
✦

We Believe

On the cross, Jesus gave his life for all his friends. At Mass, we remember his sacrifice and celebrate it.

The Great Sacrifice

The night before he died, Jesus and his friends came together for a special meal, the Last Supper.

Jesus was happy to be with his friends. But everyone knew that Jesus was in danger. Some people were even plotting to kill him.

At the meal, Jesus told them, "You are my friends. The greatest love you can show is to give your life for your friends."

Jesus then took bread into his hands. He thanked God for it. He broke the bread and gave it to his friends. "Take this and eat it," Jesus said. "This is my body. I give it up for you."

Then Jesus took a cup of wine. He thanked God for it. He gave the cup to each of his friends. "This is the cup of my blood," Jesus said. "I am ready to shed it for all of you."

They all ate and drank. "Do this in memory of me," Jesus said.

The next day, Jesus died on a cross. He gave his life for all his friends, including us. There is no greater gift than that.

Based on Matthew 26:20–30; 27–50

The New Life of Jesus

On the third day after Jesus died, God raised Jesus to new life. The risen Christ shares himself and his new life with us and all people.

Activity

Fill in the missing words for each sentence.

Jesus gave the gift of his _____ for us.

We remember his _____ and give thanks.

Signs of Love

At Mass we remember how much Jesus loves us. We remember how Jesus gave his life for us. We remember how he rose to new life. We celebrate his gift of himself to us in the Eucharist.

We remember Jesus' sacrifice during the Liturgy of the Eucharist. The priest says, "Let us proclaim the mystery of faith."

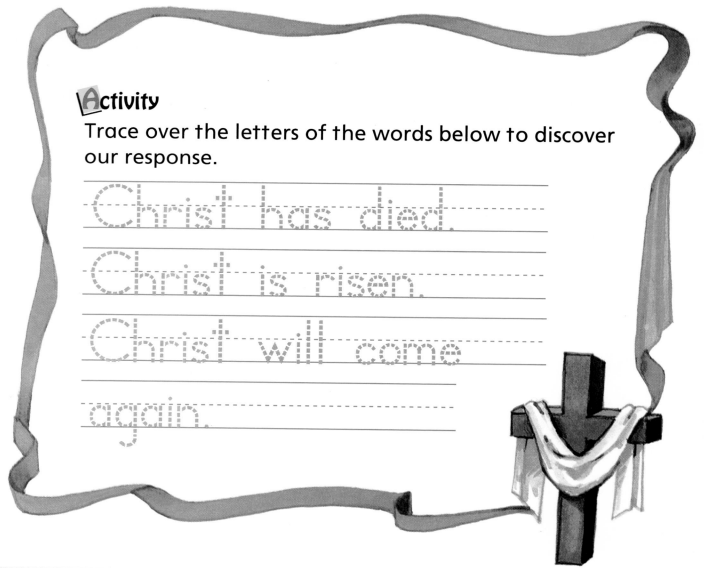

Activity

Trace over the letters of the words below to discover our response.

Christ has died.

Christ is risen.

Christ will come again.

By remembering and celebrating Jesus' sacrifice, we can become more willing to make sacrifices for others.

For You

You didn't ask me for the shell,
But I gave it to you anyway.
It was my very favorite thing,
I found it near the bay.

It may not seem like very much,
But it means a lot to me.
I gave this gift to show my love,
And I gave it willingly.

Activity

Think of something special that you could sacrifice to show your love for someone. Draw yourself offering the gift to the person.

Activity

Put a check [✔] in front of the names of places where you have seen a cross.

_____ in your home

_____ in your parish church

_____ in your classroom

_____ on a chain around someone's neck

_____ in a car

_____ in someone else's house

_____ on a building

_____ (other) _____

The Cross Is a Christian Sign

The cross is a sign that reminds us of the sacrifice of Jesus. It marks us as followers of Jesus. Christians all over the world place the cross in their homes and in their churches. We use the cross in gesture and in prayer. We pray the **Sign of the Cross** when we give and receive special blessings.

ctivity

Draw a picture of this special Christian sign.

In the name
    of the Father,
and of the Son,
and of the Holy Spirit.
    Amen.

New Word

★
★
★ **Sign of the Cross**   the prayer and gesture that marks us as
★   followers of Jesus

Praying the Sign of the Cross

Teacher: The cross of Jesus is a sign that marks us as followers of Jesus. The cross reminds us that we should be willing to sacrifice for others. When we sacrifice to help someone, we celebrate the life, death, and rising of Jesus.

We trace the sign of the cross on our foreheads.
May this sign of Jesus' love help us understand his teachings and follow him.

All: Amen.

Teacher: We trace the sign of the cross on our ears.
May we hear the voice of Jesus calling us to help others.

All: Amen.

Teacher: We trace the sign of the cross on our eyes.
May Jesus, the Light of the World, help us see the needs of others more clearly.

All: Amen.

Teacher: We trace the sign of the cross on our hands.
May we use our hands to help others.

All: Amen.

Chapter Review

Decorate and color the banner.

JESUS GIVES HIS LIFE FOR ME

1. What word describes what we do when we give something out of love?

_____

- - - - - - - - - - - - - - - - - - - -

_____

2. When do we remember and celebrate the sacrifice of Jesus?

_____

- - - - - - - - - - - - - - - - - - - -

_____

3. Talk about one sacrifice that you will make this week to show your love for someone.

Forgive each other just as the Lord has forgiven you.
Based on
Colossians 3:13

16

Jesus Is the Bread of Life

Sometimes we feel hungry but nothing we eat or drink helps. What are some of the things we need besides food?

Hungry for Comfort

Rita's class at school had a pet hamster named Squeaky. Every morning, Rita made sure that Squeaky had enough food and fresh water. Rita and Squeaky were good friends.

One morning Squeaky's cage was empty. Rita's teacher explained, "When I cleaned the cage last night, Squeaky escaped. I'm sorry, boys and girls, I know how much you loved Squeaky."

After school that day, Rita went home and sat in the kitchen. She was very quiet. "What's wrong, Rita?" her mother asked. "Do you need something to eat?"

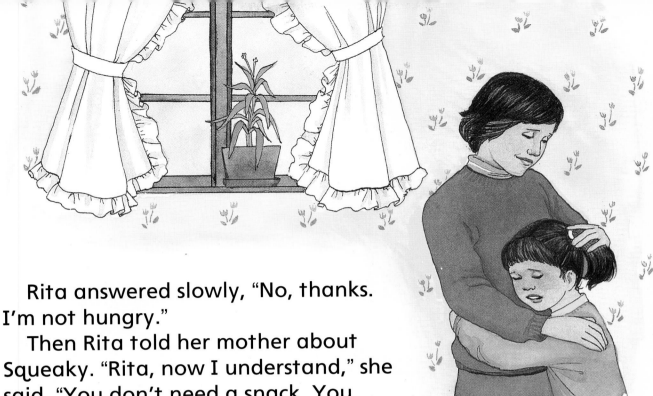

Rita answered slowly, "No, thanks. I'm not hungry."

Then Rita told her mother about Squeaky. "Rita, now I understand," she said. "You don't need a snack. You need someone to comfort you."

Mother gave Rita a hug. After that, Rita felt better.

Jesus Gives Himself to Us

Everyone needs to feel special and to belong. At Mass, Jesus gives himself to us in the **Eucharist**. We feel special because Jesus is with us in this special way. At **Communion**, we receive Jesus.

We Believe

Jesus gives us himself in the Eucharist. The Eucharist we receive at Communion is more than ordinary food and drink. In the Eucharist, Jesus gives us himself, the Bread of Life.

New Words

◆
◆
◆ **Eucharist**   Jesus' gift of himself to us at Mass
◆ **Communion**   Communion is a part of the Liturgy of the
◆   Eucharist. At Communion, Jesus gives himself
◆   to us in the Eucharist.
◆

The Bread of Life

Remember the crowd of people who listened to Jesus all day and by evening was very hungry? On that day, Jesus gave them bread and fish.

The next day the crowd was still following Jesus. They asked him for more food, but Jesus did not feed them. He spoke to them about other kinds of hunger and about other kinds of food.

Jesus said, "You should be looking for God's bread. This bread gives life to the world."

"Give us this bread," the people begged. "I am that bread," Jesus said. "I myself am the Bread of Life. If you come to me, I will fill all your hungers and thirsts."

Based on John 6:11–35

Activity

Finish the prayer. Then pray the prayer aloud with your class or quietly to yourself.

Jesus, Bread of Life,
To those who are hungry, you give food.
To those who have sinned, you give forgiveness.
To those who have no friends, you say, "Welcome!"

_____

- -

Jesus, I hunger for _____ .
Hear my prayer. Amen.

We Answer, "Amen"

We receive the Eucharist because we love Jesus, the Bread of Life, who is food for all our hungers. We also receive Eucharist because Jesus, the Bread of Life, strengthens us to care for the needs and hungers of others.

At Communion, we may choose to receive Jesus in our hand or on our tongue. As we are receiving Jesus, the priest or the eucharistic minister says to each of us, "The Body of Christ." Each of us then answers, "Amen." Our answer means, "Yes, we believe in you, Jesus. You are the Bread of Life."

Activity

Jesus gives himself to us in the Eucharist.
Fill in the words to complete this sentence.

_____

We say _____ when we receive

_____

_____ .

How will you receive Jesus in the Eucharist? Draw
yourself receiving Eucharist.

The Gift of Bread

Bread is an important part of our lives. We eat it toasted in the morning. We spread peanut butter and jelly on it for sandwiches at lunch time. For dinner, we often eat dinner rolls or garlic bread.

Here is the story of how ordinary bread is made.

▲ **1.** We mix together all the ingredients in a large bowl. As we mix the ingredients together, they become the dough.

▲ **2.** Now we are ready to knead the dough. Then the dough is ready to be put into baking pans.

4. After the dough rises, it is ready to be put into the oven to bake. ▶

▲ **3.** Yeast helps the dough rise into loaves of bread. The dough must be kept warm as it rises.

▲ **5.** The bread is baked to a golden brown. We slice the loaves of bread and enjoy their wonderful aroma and taste.

Jesus knew how important bread is in our lives. He is the Bread of Life. Here is the story of how hosts are made.

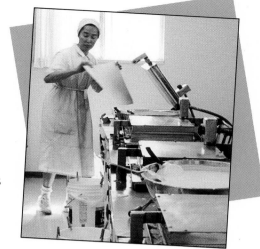

3. When the flat sheet of dough is baked, Sister removes it from the machine. ▶

▲ **1.** Sister is mixing the ingredients in a very large mixing bowl. An electric mixer is helping her mix together the flour and water.

◀ **4.** Now it is ready to be placed in another machine. This machine puts moisture into the crisp sheet of dough.

▲ **2.** Sister is spreading the thin batter on a machine that will bake the batter into a flat sheet of dough.

▲ **5.** The next morning, Sister cuts both large and small hosts with a cutting machine.

Praying About the Gift of Bread

Teacher: God has blessed us with the gift of bread. Bread fills our hunger for food. The Eucharist fills our hunger for Jesus. Let us pray together about this special gift.

Reader 1: May this loaf of bread remind us to share our bread with those who have none.

All: Blessed be God forever!

Reader 2: May this dish of unblessed hosts remind us to come often to the table of the Lord to receive Jesus, the Bread of Life.

All: Blessed be God forever!

Teacher: God, our Father, you give us everything that is good. Thank you for the gift of bread and especially for Jesus, your greatest gift.

All: Amen.

Chapter Review

Circle the word hidden in each line.
Then write these words on the lines
below the puzzle.

P	X	J	E	S	U	S
I	S	R	Y	M	N	T
P	T	H	E	L	B	T
J	O	B	R	E	A	D
X	I	N	D	M	O	F
G	L	I	F	E	S	U

_____

- - - - - - - - - - - - - - - - -

_____

- - - - - - - - - - - - - - - - -

1. Who is the Bread of Life?

_____

- - - - - - - - - - - - - - - - -

_____

2. In the Mass, when does Jesus give
himself to us?

_____

- - - - - - - - - - - - - - - - -

_____

3. Talk about what we can do to help
another person who is sad, worried,
or lonely.

**Jesus says, "I
myself am the
bread of life."**
Based on John 6:35

UNIT 4 ORGANIZER

Liturgy of the Eucharist

Bringing Up the Gifts

We respond:
_____
_____
_____
_____

Eucharistic Prayer

We respond:
_____
_____
_____
_____
_____
_____
_____
_____

Communion

We respond:
_____
_____

UNIT 4 REVIEW

Look at the words in the box. Use the correct word to finish each sentence.

| wine | altar | praise | thanks | ourselves |

1. The Liturgy of the Eucharist begins as we prepare the _____ _____.

2. We bring bread and _____ to be used in our special meal.

3. When we bring our gifts to the altar, we also bring _____ _____.

4. The Eucharist is a celebration of _____.

5. At Mass we _____ and thank God for many gifts.

UNIT **4** REVIEW

Match the priest's prayers at Mass with our responses.
Draw a line from the prayer to the correct response.

Priest

6. Let us give thanks
to the Lord our God.

7. Let us proclaim
the mystery of faith.

8. The Body of Christ.

All

Christ has died.
Christ is risen.
Christ will come again.

Amen.

It is right to give him
thanks and praise.

Circle the correct answer.

9. To sacrifice is always easy.

       Yes   No

10. At Mass we remember Jesus sacrificing his life for us.

       Yes   No

11. We can be hungry for something that is not food.

       Yes   No

12. At Communion, Jesus gives himself to us in the Eucharist.

       Yes   No

WHEN SHOULD I EXPRESS MY FEELINGS?

A good time to express my feelings is when the other person is able to pay attention to what I am saying. The other person is able to pay attention when he or she is feeling calm and is not too busy doing other things. A good time to express feelings is when the other person is ready to listen.

Activity

Look at the pictures and tell if the person in each picture is ready or not ready to listen to someone's feelings.

Ready to Listen   Not Ready to Listen

Ready to Listen   Not Ready to Listen

Ready to Listen   Not Ready to Listen

Ready to Listen   Not Ready to Listen

What should I do if someone is not ready to listen to my feelings?

If a person is not ready to listen to my feelings, I can wait until the person is ready, or I can tell someone else.

Activity

Expressing Feelings When I Have a Problem

It is important to express my feelings when I have a problem. By sharing my feelings with someone I trust, I can get help to solve my problem. I can also tell the person who is causing the problem how I feel.

Print the name of a person you can trust on the line below.

_____

Following Jesus

Jesus is always ready to listen to my feelings. Telling Jesus about my feelings is a way of praying.

A Prayer

Jesus, I love you. You are my friend. I know I can always tell you my feelings. I can always tell you my problems. You are always ready to listen. Thank you, Jesus, for loving me. Amen.

OPENING DOORS

A Take-Home Magazine™

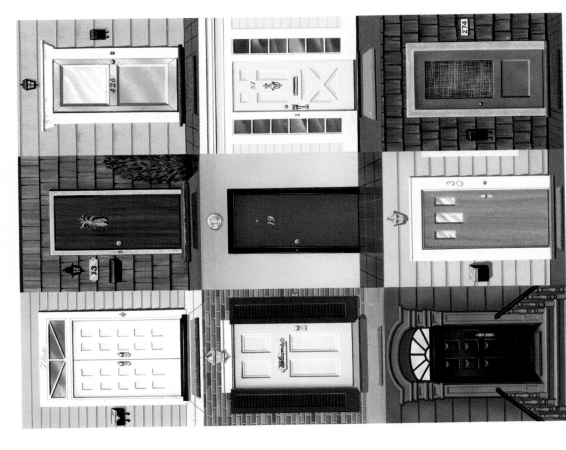

THIS IS OUR FAITH

Growing Closer

Make a special effort this week to be grateful to one another. Remember to say thanks for every kindness you experience.

Write a family prayer of thanks for all of the special people, places, and times you have shared together. Pray this prayer at meals or bedtime.

Answers for pages 4-5: family, snow, friend, God, church, Jesus; sacrifice

Looking Ahead

In Unit 5 your child will be introduced to the concept of the mystery that is the sacramental presence of Jesus in the Eucharist. He or she will focus on the Eucharist as communion—union with Jesus and others in him. Unit 5 will emphasize that those who are united to Jesus in the Eucharist are called to live according to his example.

8

2

The Generosity of God

"If you come to me,
I will fill all your hungers and thirsts."
(Adapted from John 6:34)

People who expect nothing will never be disappointed, so the saying goes. But one needs only to look at Jesus in the gospels to see that our God is a God of surprise and often gives us more than we could ever ask for or expect.

Jesus' ability to transform our simple requests into miracles and the gifts we bring to the altar into lifegiving gifts calls for more than a simple "thank you."

In the gospel accounts, we witness a few loaves and fishes multiplied to feed thousands, lepers not only helped but also completely healed, and hunger and thirst satisfied so completely that one will never again be hungry or thirsty.

Such generosity calls us to a much larger response. While we know that Eucharist means "to give thanks," we observe that the Eucharistic Prayer is more than this. When

learn that people and their needs are more important than rules, customs, and proper etiquette. Finally, the Last Supper and the resurrection meal show the sacramental dimension of meals: *when people share a meal of love and friendship, Jesus himself is present.*

Jesus understood the significance of a meal and all its implications. Giving himself under the appearances of bread and wine—made real for his followers then, and for us now, the presence of the One in whose memory this special meal was to be shared.

Forgiveness and understanding, sharing and generosity, listening to others and attending to their needs—these are all expressions of Christian spirituality. It's no wonder that the Mass, the eucharistic meal, is the center of Catholic life. We praise God when we gather in love around the altar. Jesus lives in us when we are truly present to one another; we are nourished, nurtured, and filled with new life.

the priest prays, "Let us give thanks to the Lord our God" we respond, "It is right to give him thanks *and praise.*" Knowing just how generously God provides for us, we recognize that God deserves more than mere thanks and we acknowledge our need to praise God for everything that is good.

There can be no greater investment than to bring our needs and our gifts to the Lord as we do in each eucharistic celebration. When we do this, our needs are filled and our gifts are returned to us many times over. Most especially, the gifts of bread and wine come back to us as the Bread of Life and the Cup of Salvation. In expressing our gratitude in the Eucharistic Prayer, we acknowledge the generosity of our God and confidently expect to be renewed and transformed into the Body of Christ.

Being Catholic

Meals in the Bible

Eating a certain amount of food each day is essential to human existence. Meals, however, have always provided more than basic nourishment for those who shared them.

In biblical times, the Jews ate only two meals a day. The chief meal was eaten between 3 and 4 P.M., but it often lasted until nightfall. The most important meal of the year was the Passover meal—the ritual meal of lamb, bitter herbs, wine, and unleavened bread, which commemorated the flight of the Jews from Egypt.

Here are a few of the meals recorded in the gospels.
- Jesus shares a meal at Simon's house (Mt. 26:6–13).
- The multiplication of loaves (Mt. 14:19; 15:35).
- Jesus eats a meal with Zacchaeus (Lk. 19:1–10).
- Jesus eats a meal with Martha and Mary (Lk. 10:30–42).
- Jesus works his first miracle at a wedding banquet (Jn. 2:1–11).
- The Emmaus meal (Lk. 24:13–35).

From these examples, it is clear that meals can have more than a physical or social function. Meals can have a spiritual dimension as well.

At the suppers with Simon and Zacchaeus, Jesus forgives someone. In the stories about the multiplication of loaves and the wedding feast of Cana, sharing and generosity emerge as important virtues. From the meal with Martha and Mary, we

God's Great Gifts

Recount with your child the many gifts and blessings your family has enjoyed. Teach your child the prayer response from the Mass, "It is right to give you thanks and praise." Enjoy the riddles on these pages with your child.

At Mass we praise and thank God for many gifts. We remember Jesus and the new life he shares with us. We thank Jesus for the wonderful gift of Eucharist.

Try these riddles. Discover some of God's gifts to you.

We love you more than anyone else. We take care of you every day. You made us very happy the day you were born. Who are we?

m (a) f y (i) l

I make the earth look beautiful in winter. I lay a soft, fluffy blanket of white everywhere. I am fun to play in. What am I?

o (s) w n

I like to play with you. We spend fun times together. We help one another and share secrets. Who am I?

n d (i) e (r) f

I made you because I love you. I give you everything you need and people who take care of you. Who am I?

o d (G)

We are the people of God. We are followers of Jesus. Our building has the same name as us. Who are we?

r h (c) u (c) h

I give myself to you in the Eucharist. I died on the cross for you. I share new life with you. Who am I?

(e) s J s u

Now unscramble the circled letters to complete the sentence below.

At Mass we remember the _____ of Jesus and give thanks.

Thank Jesus for the gift of Eucharist the next time you go to Mass. Pray the prayer of thanks and praise you learned today. Celebrate God's love for you!

UNIT 5

The Eucharist Is Jesus with Us

Who is one person you always like to be with?

The Eucharist Unites Us

A Class Project

One day, Mr. Jackson carried a large box into the second-grade classroom. He put the box on his desk and began to pull out small pieces of cloth. He told the class, "This week we are going to work together on a class art project."

Mr. Jackson explained what they were going to do. "I'm going to give each of you a large cloth patch," he said. "I'm also going to give you scissors, glue, and some smaller pieces of cloth. Each of you can cut out a shape. Then I'll help you glue it on the large patch. When you have finished your patches, we will sew them together to make one big quilt."

The children worked on their patches for two days. Then it was time to work together to form all the patches into a quilt. The children worked together peacefully and helped one another.

Tell about a project you worked on with other people.

When the quilt was finished, Mr. Jackson hung it on the classroom wall.

"What a beautiful quilt we've made," Mr. Jackson said. "Because we worked together, all the individual patches now form one special quilt."

We Can Work Together

To make the quilt, everyone in Mr. Jackson's second grade class had to work together peacefully. Each person helped make the project special.

Jesus wants us to work together and live together in peace. This is not always easy. Jesus gives himself to us in the Eucharist to help us live together in peace and **unity**.

We Believe

The Eucharist is a sacrament of peace and unity. In this sacrament, Jesus helps us to become friends with all people and to be united in peace and love.

New Word

* unity   joined together in peace

Jesus Prays for His Friends

On the night before Jesus died, his friends talked with him as they ate and drank. They shared the bread of life Jesus gave them. They felt very close to Jesus and to one another.

Jesus hoped that his friends would always be together as they were that night. But Jesus knew how people sometimes think only of themselves. He knew how hard it is for friends always to work well with one another and feel close to one another.

So Jesus prayed. "Father, help my friends to be happy together. Unite them in peace and love. Help them to be as close to one another as you and I are.

"Father, I pray for all those who become my friends. Help them to be united as friends. I pray that they may all be one."

Activity

1. Underline the sentence that tells what Jesus hoped for his friends.

2. Draw a box around the prayer Jesus prayed for his friends.

3. Write a short prayer for your friends. Use the lines below.

The Prayer of Jesus

Jesus' first friends and followers knew that Jesus often prayed to God, our Father. They noticed, too, that Jesus prayed in a very special way. He called God "Abba." In the language Jesus spoke, Abba means "Daddy." They asked Jesus to teach them to pray. Jesus taught them the prayer that we now call The Lord's Prayer. All Christians pray the prayer that Jesus taught.

The Lord's Prayer

Our Father, who art in heaven,
   hallowed be thy name;
thy kingdom come;
thy will be done on earth
   as it is in heaven.
Give us this day our daily bread;
and forgive us our trespasses
   as we forgive those
   who trespass against us;
and lead us not into temptation,
   but deliver us from evil.
Amen.

Together in Peace

Jesus asks all who receive the Eucharist to live together in unity and peace.

At Mass we show our unity by singing and praying together and by standing, sitting, and kneeling together. Before we receive the Eucharist, we show our unity by praying the prayer that Jesus taught us.

After we pray The Lord's Prayer at Mass, we pray:

Priest: The peace of the Lord be with you always.
All: And also with you.
Priest: Let us offer each other a sign of peace.

Then we reach out to those around us, shake their hands, kiss or hug them, and wish them peace.

Activity

Tell how you wish peace to others at Mass.

Activity

What does peace look like to you? Draw it here.

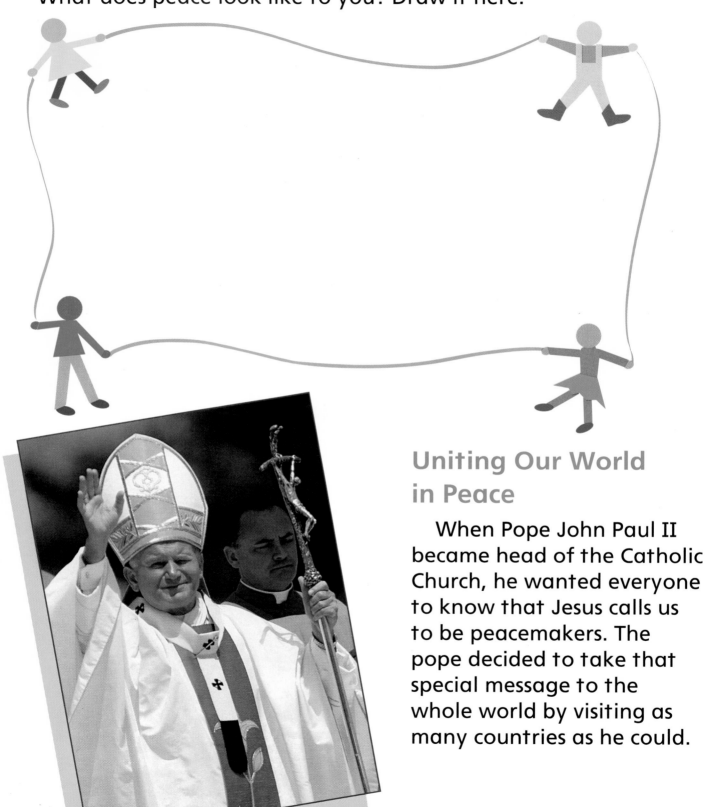

Uniting Our World in Peace

When Pope John Paul II became head of the Catholic Church, he wanted everyone to know that Jesus calls us to be peacemakers. The pope decided to take that special message to the whole world by visiting as many countries as he could.

On one of his trips to the United States, the pope met with thousands of young people. The young people were from all over the world. The pope celebrated Mass with them. He asked them to be followers of Jesus. He asked them to take peace and unity back to their families and parishes.

Activity

Put a ✔ in front of some ways you might choose to bring peace and unity to your home, neighborhood, and school.

_____ Cooperate in school

_____ Do my chores without being reminded

_____ Let others have their way sometimes

_____ Play fairly on my sports team

_____ Respect my brothers' and sisters' things

_____ Pray for people who make me angry

_____ Not fight with my friends or family

Praying with Dance

Teacher: Let us pray today by dancing a dance of peace.

Peace before us.

Peace behind us.

Peace under our feet.

Peace within us.

Peace over us.

Let all around us be peace.

Chapter Review

Put a **T** by each sentence below that is true.

_____ Jesus prayed that his friends would be happy and always united.

_____ Jesus does not want us to work together in peace and love.

_____ In the Eucharist, Jesus helps us to be united and to work in peace.

_____ We should not pray for our friends.

1. What did Jesus pray for on the night before he died?

   _____

   _____

   _____

   _____

2. What word means "joined together in peace"?

   _____

   _____

All who eat the bread of life are one.
Based on
1 Corinthians 10:17

3. Talk about what we can do as friends and followers of Jesus that shows we care about other people and are ready to be peacemakers.

The Eucharist Calls Us to Serve

Activity

Read the sentences near the pictures. Talk about the different kinds of help we can give to other people.

◀ The children are welcoming a new student. They want him to feel a part of their class.

Devon enjoys spending time with his grandfather. Devon's grandfather likes teaching him how to hit a baseball. ▶

Tell a story about something you said or did that helped another person.

◀ Linda, Tracy, and Maria are helping each other with a school project.

Jesus Wants Us to Help

Jesus wants his friends always to love and **serve** all people. He wants us to treat other people the way he treated them. At Mass we remember that Jesus asked us to serve one another. The Eucharist helps us reach out with love and kindness to other people, especially to those who are in need.

Activity

Think about the different kinds of help you give to others every day. List them here.

_____

_____

_____

_____

Think about the kinds of help others give you every day. List them here.

_____

_____

_____

_____

We Believe

The Eucharist is a sacrament of love and service. Those who share the Bread of Life are asked to care for everyone.

New Word

✳
✳ **serve**   to help others and to be kind to them
✳

Activity

How are these people helping others?

_____

- -

_____

Love and Serve

At the end of Mass, the priest sends us forth with a blessing. He reminds us that what we just celebrated together strengthens us to love and serve God. We do this by helping and caring for all God's people.

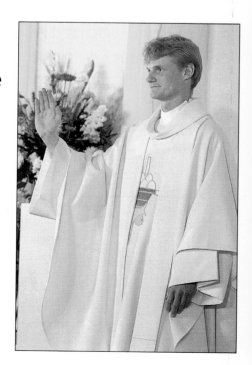

Priest: May almighty God bless you, the Father, and the Son, ✠ and the Holy Spirit.

All: Amen.

Priest: Go in peace to love and serve the Lord.

All: Thanks be to God.

Activity

When we leave Mass, we can begin to love and serve others at home, at school, and in our neighborhoods. Choose a word from the picture to complete the prayer below.

When someone is sad,
Lord Jesus, help me to bring _____.

When someone hurts me,
Lord Jesus, help me to _____.

When someone feels lonely,
Lord Jesus, help me to be a _____.

When someone fights,
Lord Jesus, help me to bring _____.

To Love and Serve ~~~~~~~

It was the night before Jesus died. He and his friends were gathered together to share a very special meal. Jesus had many things to teach his friends that night.

At the meal, Jesus stood up and walked across the room. He picked up a bowl of water and a towel. He carried them back to the table.

Jesus knelt down in front of his friends. He began to wash their feet. When he came to Peter, Peter said, "Jesus, I should be washing your feet. You should not be washing mine."

No one in the room understood why Jesus was doing what servants always did for guests. So when Jesus was finished washing his friends' feet, he explained. "I have given you an example," he said. "You must serve others, as I have served you."

Based on John 13:1–17

Activity

Use the code to find a message from Jesus.

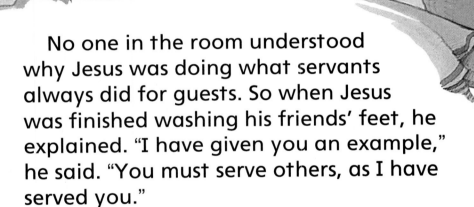

a	e	h	x	o	r	s	t	v	m	p	d
1	2	3	4	5	6	7	8	9	10	11	12

g	i	n	y	f	l
13	14	15	16	17	18

$\overline{10}\ \overline{16}\quad \overline{17}\ \overline{6}\ \overline{14}\ \overline{2}\ \overline{15}\ \overline{12}\ \overline{7}\ '\ \overline{7}\ \overline{2}\ \overline{6}\ \overline{9}\ \overline{2}\quad \overline{5}\ \overline{15}\ \overline{2}$

$\overline{1}\ \overline{15}\ \overline{5}\ \overline{8}\ \overline{3}\ \overline{2}\ \overline{6}\quad \overline{14}\ \overline{15}\quad \overline{18}\ \overline{5}\ \overline{9}\ \overline{2}$

Search and Rescue

Darryl and Peggy know what it means to serve others. This husband and wife are rescuers—persons who search for and rescue people who are missing because of earthquakes or other disasters.

Darryl and Peggy have been rescuing injured or missing people since they first met each other ten years ago. They have traveled around the world, helping local police officers and firefighters find people who may be trapped or badly injured inside buildings or under bridges.

Darryl and Peggy have two search dogs named Molly and Duffy. The dogs have been specially trained to sniff their way through a fallen building or other dangerous area until they pick up the scent of a child or grown-up who is trapped.

When Molly and Duffy find an injured person, they let Darryl and Peggy know that someone is trapped by barking and scratching at the ground. Darryl and Peggy then let the rescue people know where to start digging so that the person can be brought to safety.

Darryl and Peggy serve many, many people by using their time and their talents to help others in a very special way. They show us that all Jesus' followers can serve others by using the gifts and talents God has given us.

Activity

Draw a picture of or write about one special way you can serve others by using your gifts and talents.

Praying About Serving Jesus

All: Jesus, how can we serve you?

Child #1: You can serve me by visiting those who are sick or old.

All: Jesus, how can we serve you?

Child #2: You can serve me by giving food to those who are hungry.

All: Jesus, how can we serve you?

Child #3: You can serve me by welcoming people to your home or school.

All: Jesus, how can we serve you?

Child #4: You can serve me by using your gifts and talents to help others.

Teacher: Jesus, help us to see you in all those we serve.

All: Amen.

Chapter Review

We can love and serve other people every day.
We can help people wherever we are.
Finish each group of words below by naming
one way you can serve other people.

In school, I can

_____

- -

_____ .

At home, I can

_____

- -

_____ .

1. What word means to help people and to be
kind to them?

_____

- -

_____

2. In the gospel story we just read, how did
Jesus serve his friends?

_____

- -

_____

3. Talk about those people in your
community who give service to
other people or who help care
for the earth.

**Out of love,
place
yourselves at
one another's
service.**
Galatians 5:13

The Eucharist Is a Promise of New Life

The Changing Seasons

Brian can see his favorite oak tree from his bedroom window. The leaves turn colors, die, and fall from the trees in the autumn.

In the winter, snow covers the bare branches, and squirrels scamper for buried food.

The birds return in the spring and perch on the budding limbs.

What does being alive mean to you?

ctivity

What will Brian see when he looks at his oak tree in the summer? Draw it here.

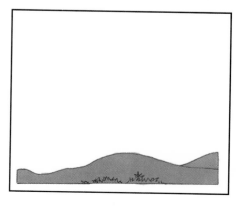

Changes in Our Lives

Life changes every day. After Jesus died, he rose to new life. Someday our lives will change in a very special way. Jesus promises that those who receive him in the Eucharist will share in his life.

Activity

Complete the message from Jesus. Use the words in the box.

life	bread	forever	eats	live

Jesus says,

_____   _____

"Whoever _____ the _____

_____   _____

of _____ will _____

_____

_____."

Activity

Your grandparents live far away. You haven't seen them for two years. Name two ways you have changed since their last visit.

_____

- -

_____

- -

_____

We Grow and Change

God makes each of us special. No two people are exactly the same. Yet every person grows and changes.

As we grow, we change in many ways. We grow taller. We learn to walk and to talk. We change from babies into toddlers and then into children. In the years ahead, we will continue to grow. We will change into teenagers and finally, into adults.

Just as people grow and change, animals and plants grow and change. God has made all living things special. God has made people most special of all.

Activity

Each of these pictures shows life changes. Circle the pictures that show something you have seen happen. Choose one of the pictures and tell your story.

New Life

Mary of Magdala was crying as she stood in front of the place where they had buried Jesus. When she looked inside, she found that it was empty.

A man was standing a few feet away from Mary. "Why are you crying?" he asked. "Whom are you looking for?"

Mary turned around. She thought the man was a gardener. "Please tell me where you have taken Jesus," Mary begged.

The man called her name again. Mary wiped her tears and saw that it was Jesus! Now Mary recognized him. "Teacher!" she shouted. She was so glad he was alive!

Then Jesus said to Mary, "I'm going to my Father and your Father, to my God and your God."

Mary knew then that someday she would be with Jesus and with God the Father. She ran back to tell Jesus' other friends the good news.

Based on John 20:11–18

The Resurrection

We, like Mary of Magdala, believe that Jesus rose to new life after his death on the cross. We call that rising to new life Jesus' **resurrection**. We also believe that we share in Jesus' resurrection. Jesus promised that all who eat the bread of life will live forever. When we die, we will share a new life with Jesus and with all who love God.

We Believe

Jesus rose from death to new life. He promises that those who eat the bread of life will live with him forever. The Eucharist is a sacrament of new life.

New Word

resurrection   Jesus' rising from death to new life

Alive with Jesus

The phone rang just as they sat down to eat dinner. Melissa got to it first, as she always did.

"Hi, Grandma!" Melissa smiled as she heard her grandmother 's voice. But soon Melissa began to cry and quickly handed the phone to her mother.

"Grandpa died," she said softly as she threw her arm around her dad's neck. Josh got out of his chair and climbed up on his father's lap.

Mr. Riós and the children held each other tight. It helped so much to be together now.

"Why did he have to die?" Josh asked.

"Grandpa had been sick for a long time. The doctors did everything they could to help him get well, but he was just too sick," Mr. Riós said.

"Death is a part of life, and we all will die someday. But death is not the end. Grandpa is alive with Jesus."

"I will miss him so much," Melissa cried. Josh said nothing, but he thought about Grandpa and about what his dad had told them.

Remember and Celebrate

When those we love die, we are sad. But we know they are alive with Jesus. At Mass we remember them and celebrate their new life. On Easter we celebrate Jesus' resurrection.

The large Easter candle that stands near the altar reminds us that all who die will live a new life with Jesus.

Activity

At Mass we express our belief in Jesus' resurrection and in his promise of new life when we say this prayer. Use the words below to complete the prayer.

resurrection	cross	world	savior	free

Lord, by your _____ and

_____,

you have set us _____.

You are the _____.

of the _____.

Praying About Time

Teacher: When we were born,
All: You were there,
God, giving us life.

Teacher: When we learned how to walk,
All: You were there,
God, giving us life.

Teacher: When we made our first friend,
All: You were there,
God, giving us life.

Teacher: When we become teenagers,
All: You'll be there, God, giving us life.

Teacher: When we get our first jobs,
All: You'll be there,
God, giving us life.

Teacher: When we die and go home to you,
All: You'll be there,
God, giving us life.

Chapter Review

Choose a word to complete each sentence.

Jesus rose from death to _____ life.

When we die, we will be with _____.

The Easter _____ reminds us of Jesus' resurrection.

1. What do we call Jesus' rising from death to new life?

_____

_____

2. What does Jesus promise those who eat the bread of life?

_____

_____

3. Talk about how we can help those who are sad because someone has died.

Jesus says,
"Whoever
eats the
bread of life will
live forever."
John 6:51

20 The Eucharist Celebrates the Presence of Jesus

Being with Others

It's good to spend time with those we love. It's good to be near people who love us.

Who are some people who enjoy spending time with you?

Sometimes we like to be alone. But we also want to know someone is near when we need him or her.

Jesus Is Always with Us

Jesus is alive and with us. Jesus is with us always and everywhere. We celebrate the presence of Jesus with us in the Eucharist.

Activity

Read the prayer below.
Then circle the names of some of the places where Jesus is with us.

O Lord,
Where can I go from your presence?
If I fly up into the sky,
You are there.
If I sink deep under the earth,
You are present there.
If I cross the widest ocean,
You are there to guide me.
Your right hand holds me tight.

Based on Psalm 139:7–10

We Believe

The Eucharist is the sacrament of the presence of Jesus. Jesus is with us in the Eucharist and always.

Jesus Is Here

Two men were walking from Jerusalem to **Emmaus**. They were very sad. "I miss Jesus so much," Cleopas said, "I wish he was here with us."

A stranger came down the road and started walking with the two men. "Why are you so sad?" the stranger asked the two men.

"We have lost our friend Jesus," Cleopas answered. "He died on a cross two days ago."

"Don't be sad!" the stranger said. "Don't you understand what has happened? Jesus had to die to lead us all to new life." Then the stranger explained the stories in the Bible about the coming of the savior.

The two friends listened carefully. What the stranger said gave them hope. "It's getting late," Cleopas said to the stranger. "We are almost home. Please stay with us tonight." Soon they were home in Emmaus. They sat down to eat. The stranger took bread in his hands. He thanked God for it.

He broke the bread and gave it to the other two. Now they knew that the stranger was Jesus.

Later Cleopas ran to tell the others, "He is alive! He is with us!"

Based on Luke 24:13–35

ctivity

Draw a picture that shows a time when you were sure that Jesus was with you.

New Word

Emmaus   the place where Jesus shared a meal with two of his followers after he rose to new life

Activity

Pretend that this is a map of your neighborhood. Begin at the START sign and follow the arrows. Stop at each place along the way and write the name of a person who is usually present to you there.

We Celebrate the Presence of Jesus

We celebrate the presence of Jesus every time we gather as a community for Mass. The risen Jesus is present at Mass with the people and priest who gather.

Jesus is also present in the Bible readings. He is present in the Eucharist we share.

Activity

During Mass the priest reminds us that Jesus is present with us. Write our response on the line below.

Priest: The Lord be with you.

All: _____

Faces! Faces! Faces!

Everyone has a face. Faces can be friendly, angry, mean, or sad. We like to remember the faces of people we love.

Activity

Whose face do you like to remember most?

_____

- -

_____

Now draw that person's face in the box.

Jesus Has Many Faces

Christians around the world believe that Jesus is always with them. Many people paint pictures or make statues of Jesus to show that they believe that Jesus is always present. The paintings and statues show Jesus with many different faces, because no one really knows what Jesus looked like. Here are a few of those faces.

Activity

What do you think Jesus' face looks like?
Draw it here.

Praying About the Presence of Jesus

Teacher: Jesus is present in many ways. Let us think about Jesus' presence within us. Let us visit with him there.

Jesus, we know that you are always close to us. You are as close to us as the air we breathe. With each breath, we thank you for being our friend.

Jesus, we know that you live in our hearts. The beating of our hearts reminds us that you stay with us every minute of every day.

Jesus, your love for us fills our minds. We can remember you. We can pray to you. We can speak to you. We can listen to you. We can love you.

Jesus, thank you for being so close to us. Even when we forget you, you never forget us. You never leave us. Help us stay close to you always.

All: Amen!

Chapter Review

Read the sentences below.
Circle **YES** if a sentence is true.
Circle **NO** if a sentence is not true.

1. Jesus is with the Christian community.

       YES   NO

2. Presence means "being alone."

       YES   NO

3. Jesus is not with us anymore.

       YES   NO

4. Jesus is with us in the Eucharist.

       YES   NO

5. Jesus is with us in the Bible readings at Mass.

       YES   NO

1. In the story "Jesus Is Here," when did the two followers recognize Jesus?

_____

- -

_____

2. When is Jesus, the risen Christ, with us?

_____

- -

_____

Jesus says,
"I am with you always."
Matthew 28:20

3. Talk about how we can help ourselves and others remember that Jesus is always with us.

UNIT **5** ORGANIZER

The Eucharist Is Jesus with Us
Draw your pictures below.

This is my picture of what unity in Jesus <u>tastes</u> like.

This is my picture of what serving others <u>feels</u> like.

This is my picture of what new life in Jesus <u>sounds</u> like.

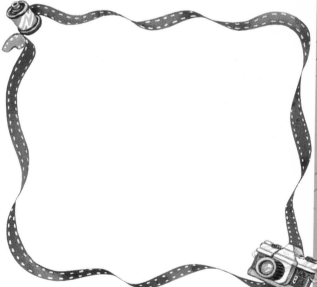

This is my picture of what the Emmaus meal <u>looks</u> like.

252 Unit Organizer

UNIT **5** REVIEW

Circle the correct answer.

1. Jesus wants us to work _____.

                apart   together

2. Jesus prayed for his friends to be _____.

                united   poor

3. At Mass we give each other a sign of _____.

                danger   peace

Look at the words in the box. Then write the correct word to complete each sentence.

treat   example   peace

4. Jesus washed his friends' feet to give us an

_____

_____ of how to serve others.

5. The Eucharist is a sacrament of love and _____.

6. Jesus wants us to _____ others the way he did.

UNIT **5** REVIEW

Talk about the answers
to the following questions.

7. What did Jesus
   promise those who
   eat the bread of life?

8. What do Christians believe happens
   after someone dies?

9. What does the Easter candle remind us of at Mass?

Think about the story "Jesus Is Here." Write your answer to
each question.

10. What happened when Cleopas and his friend ate
    supper with the stranger?

    _____

    -

    _____

11. When and where is Jesus with us?

    _____

    -

    _____

WHAT SHOULD I DO WHEN MY MESSAGE ISN'T HEARD?

Sometimes my message is not heard. Sometimes my message is heard but not understood.

Activity

Meet Larry. Larry is a new student in the second grade. Larry is having a hard time fitting in. The other kids tease Larry. Larry feels

_____

- -

_____ .

Larry decides to tell his dad. His dad is watching a football game. Larry says, "Dad, I hate school. The kids are being mean." His dad says, "You'll like it after you're there a while. Wow! Look at that touchdown!"

Was Larry's message heard?

Yes   No

Was Larry's message understood?

Yes   No

What should Larry do?

Larry decides to try again later. This time he waits for a time when his dad is ready to listen. Larry says, "Dad, I hate school. The kids are being mean." His dad says, "You sound really sad. Do you want to tell me more about it?"

Was Larry's message heard?

Yes   No

Was Larry's message understood?

Yes   No

Upset, scared, and worried feelings are important feelings to share with someone who will listen. Don't give up if your message isn't heard.

Following Jesus

Jesus understands what it feels like to be upset, scared, and worried. He sometimes felt those same feelings. Jesus wants us to share all our feelings with him and with someone else we trust.

A Prayer

Jesus, sometimes I need someone to listen to my feelings when I'm upset or scared. I know you always listen to me. Thank you, Jesus! Amen.

OPENING DOORS
A Take-Home Magazine™

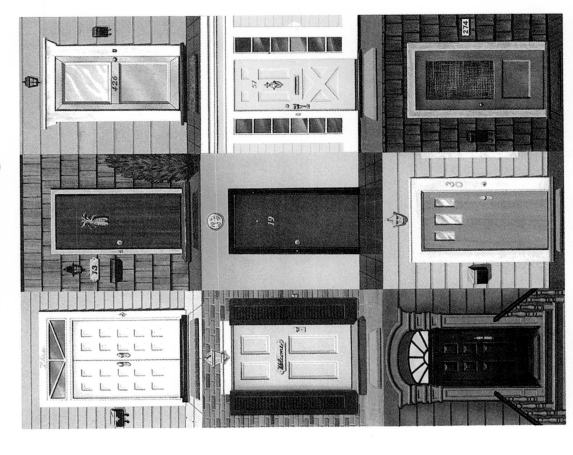

THIS IS OUR FAITH

Growing Closer

TALK TOGETHER about what *sacrifice* means. Decide on one sacrifice your family could make this week. One example might be spending a few hours doing yard work for an elderly or handicapped person in your neighborhood or parish.

BE REALLY PRESENT to your family this week. Listen to one another. Spend some time together. Do something nice for your family for no reason at all!

Looking Ahead

However your family spends the summer, may it be a time of renewal and recreation, good health and happiness, joyful celebrations, and an opportunity to relax in the promise, "I am with you always" (Mt. 28:20).

"Bring together in love and peace all who believe in you."
—Roman Missal

A Builder of Unity

Today we understand the Mass as an important builder of unity among Catholics. It also stands as a sign of the unified body of Christ fully alive in the world today. As we are often reminded in the Mass, we not only gather to receive the body of Christ but we are also sent forth to be the body of Christ. Working together and making sacrifices for one another, we know that it is through our lives and the life of the Church that Jesus is made known to the people around us in a profound way. Without question, this is a great responsibility, but living and expressing our faith within a community of believers is a great gift, too!

- Augustus Tolton was the first recognized black priest in the United States. He was ordained in 1886 and sent to work with black Catholics in Illinois.

- Lincoln Valle and Daniel Rudd, two prominent black newspapermen, founded a series of Black Catholic Congresses (1889–1894). The congresses called for more Catholic schools, orphanages, and hospitals for blacks.

- Thomas Wyatt Turner (1877–1978), a professor at Howard University, organized the Federated Colored Catholics, an organization that sought to end racial discrimination.

3

It was during Jesus' last days on earth that we find him praying for the unity of his friends and followers, showing us how to serve one another, and speaking of the way of love as a way of sacrifice. These things seemed to be of great value to Jesus.

The Mass as a source of unity helps us as Jesus' followers to align our values with the values of Jesus. We are challenged to serve one another. We are encouraged to walk the way of love, perhaps at great sacrifice to ourselves. And we are called to forgiveness and to faithfulness.

Through it all, the Mass reminds us that our faith journey is never a journey we take alone. Jesus is present to us throughout the journey, encouraging and guiding us through the Spirit and also by means of the community gathered around the eucharistic table.

Black Catholic Contributions

Since the early years of the Church, black Catholics have embraced Catholicism with unswerving faith and dedication.

Did you know

- that North Africa was a flourishing center of the early Church?
- that many of the early monks and nuns were black?
- that one of these, Saint Moses the Black, was a great spiritual leader in the early fifth century?

Here is a brief list that will help acquaint you with some of the contributions black Catholics have made throughout the Church's history.

- Saint Benedict the Black (1526–1589) was a Franciscan friar and spiritual leader in Sicily, around Palermo.

- Saint Martin de Porres (1579–1639) was a Dominican friar who took care of the black slaves and the poor of Lima, Peru.

- Elizabeth Lange founded the Oblate Sisters of Providence for black women in Baltimore, 1829.

- Henriette Delille founded the Sisters of the Holy Family in New Orleans in 1842 to serve as teachers and guardians of black children.

- Pierre Toussaint (1766–1853) was a New York hairdresser who practiced remarkable charity. He is now a candidate for sainthood.

Jesus Is with Us

Every day your love and care make the presence of Jesus real for your family. At Mass we celebrate Jesus present in our lives and in the Eucharist. Help your child identify and celebrate all the moments when Jesus is present in your child's life.

Jesus is always with us. At Mass we gather together as friends. We celebrate Jesus with us. We remember how Jesus loved and served others.

When we leave Mass, we try to love and serve others as Jesus would. Jesus is always present when we care for one another.

Draw a picture on page 5 showing ways your family will try to make Jesus present to others this week.

At Mass, be aware of the special presence of Jesus in the scriptural readings and in the Eucharist. Bring that presence to everyone you live with, work with, and meet this week.

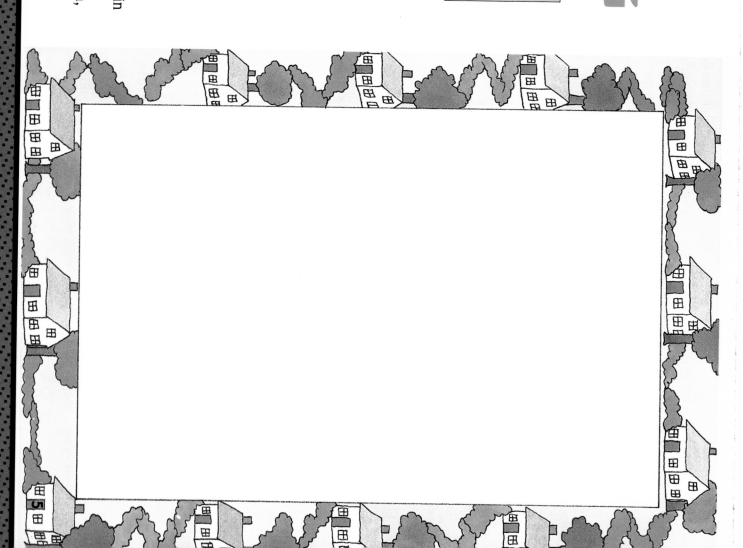

Celebrating the Journey

Leader: Many months ago we began a journey of faith together. Today we come here to recall all that we have learned and shared. We believe that Jesus is here with us and so we celebrate in the name of the Father, and of the Son, and of the Holy Spirit.

All: Amen.

Leader: Jesus, our Friend and our Savior, thank you for being with us on our journey of faith. Stay with us now as we listen carefully to your word. We ask this in your name.

All: Amen.

Reader: A reading from John's Gospel.
The gospel of the Lord.

All: Praise to you, Lord Jesus Christ.

Leader: Remembering that Jesus calls us his friends, let us offer each other a greeting of peace.

All: Amen.

Leader: Jesus, thank you for showing us God's love. Help us to share that love with one another. Keep us united with all our brothers and sisters.

All: Amen.

Our Church Celebrates Advent

A Time to Prepare

Mary had an older cousin named Elizabeth. Elizabeth and her husband, Zechariah, were lonely because they did not have any children of their own. But one day God sent a messenger to Zechariah. The messenger said, "God will send you a son. Name him John. He will help prepare for God's Son, Jesus."

Based on Luke 1:5–17

When John grew up, he was a messenger for God. He told people to prepare their hearts and minds for Jesus. He went from town to town saying, "Make ready the way of the Lord."

Based on Matthew 3:3

Activity

During Advent we get ready for Jesus to come into our lives at Christmas. We prepare our hearts for Jesus by being loving and caring.

On the lines below, write ways you can be loving and caring during Advent. Then color the banner.

1. _____

2. _____

3. _____

4. _____

5. _____

Prepare your ♥ for Jesus

The Church Prepares for Jesus' Coming

"Hurry, Kara," called Mrs. Mead. "We have to get to church." Kara ran downstairs. Her family was waiting. "We're going to light the Advent wreath today," said David, Kara's brother.

When the Meads got to Saint John Church, it was quiet. The lights were dim. A big tree decorated with paper tags stood in the corner. An Advent wreath with tall candles was near the altar.

The Mass began. Father Paul was dressed in purple vestments. He prayed for Jesus to come into their lives during Advent. Mr. Mead helped Kara light a candle on the wreath.

Later, Father Paul talked about the tags on the tree. He said that the names of families who needed food, clothes, and toys for Christmas were written on the tags. Father asked the people of the parish to take a name if they wanted to help another family.

After Mass, David ran to take a tag from the tree. "Can we help?" asked Kara.

"What a wonderful idea!" said Mrs. Mead. "Advent is a special time to think of others."

During Advent we pray, "Jesus, you bring light and joy to our lives. Help us to be signs of your light by bringing happiness to others during Advent."

Activity

Write the names of some people you will be kind to this Advent. Use the tree tags.

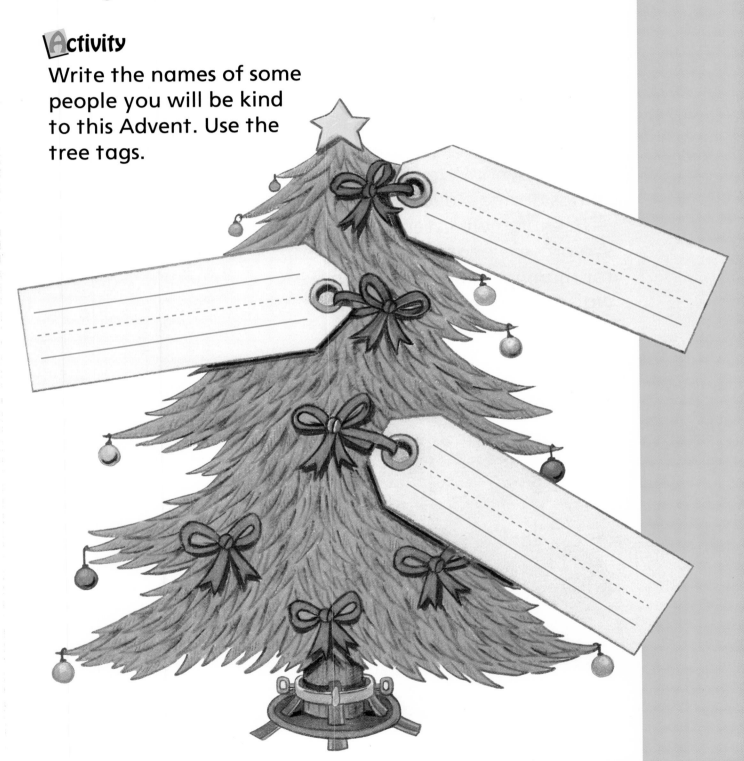

Advent in Our Lives

During Advent we prepare our hearts for Jesus. At home we can pray together. We can look for ways to be caring and loving to the people in our families.

At school we can do projects. We can collect toys for children who have none. We can secretly choose names of children in our class for whom we can do kind things during Advent.

In church we listen to God's word. We pray as people have prayed for many years while they have waited for Jesus.

At home, at school, and at church we celebrate Advent. Our words and actions say, "We are getting ready. Jesus is coming into our lives."

Activity

Circle the correct word to complete each sentence.
Then use these words to fill in the puzzle below.

1. During Advent we can do _____ acts for our friends.

          caring   selfish

2. Advent is a time to _____.

          work   pray

3. During Advent we prepare our minds and hearts
for _____.

          Jesus   Mary

4. We prepare for Christmas during _____.

          Lent   Advent

C H R I S T I A N

An Advent Reminder

Make a chalkboard to remind yourself that Advent is a time to prepare for Jesus at home, at school, and at church. These are the things you will need.

- 4 craft sticks
- 1 square sheet of black construction paper
- a white crayon
- glue
- a piece of yarn

Follow the directions your teacher gives you to make your chalkboard. When you are finished, use the crayon to write an Advent message on your board.

You can hang your chalkboard on a doorknob or a mirror. It will remind you to get ready for Jesus.

Help Us Prepare, Lord Jesus

We can ask Jesus to help us get ready for his coming into our lives at Christmas.

Teacher: With our families we can pray and be helpful.

Children: Help us prepare at home, Lord Jesus.

Teacher: With our classmates we can share and be kind.

Children: Help us prepare at school, Lord Jesus.

Teacher: With our parish we can listen and learn.

Children: Help us prepare at church, Lord Jesus.

All: We want to get ready for you, Jesus. We want you to come into our hearts and minds at Christmas. Help us prepare for your coming.

Our Church Celebrates Christmas

The Christmas Message

Shepherds were caring for their sheep in a field near Bethlehem. An angel from God appeared to them and said, "Do not be afraid. I bring you good news. Today your Savior has been born. You will find him in a manger."

The shepherds were surprised and excited. They hurried to Bethlehem. There they found Jesus in the manger. They knew that what the messenger had said was true. Their Savior was born. They were happy and told everyone the good news about Jesus.

Based on Luke 2:8–18

Activity

Use the following code to complete the Christmas message.

a	e	i	o	u	s	j	v	b	r	n
1	2	3	4	5	6	7	8	9	10	11

___ ___ ___ ___ ___, our ___ ___ ___ ___ ___ ___,
7   2   6   5   6   6   1   8   3   4   10

is ___ ___ ___ ___.
   9   4   10   11

Draw a picture of the shepherds visiting the baby Jesus.

Christmas Around the World

Christmas is celebrated everywhere. There are many Christmas traditions. **Tradition** means doing something the same way every year.

In Mexico, <u>Las Posadas</u> is a Christmas tradition. The words <u>las posadas</u> mean "the inns." Families carry lighted candles from house to house, acting out Mary and Joseph's search for a place to stay on Christmas Eve. Two people act as Mary and Joseph. They knock on a neighbor's door and ask to come in. At first the person acting as the innkeeper will not let them in. Joseph asks again. Finally they are welcomed into the house. Inside, everyone sings Christmas carols. The children break open a piñata, a paper or clay decoration filled with candy.

In Ireland, families put lighted candles in their front windows to welcome travelers. This helps the people to remember Mary and Joseph's journey to Bethlehem.

Do you have a Christmas crib under your tree? Saint Francis began this tradition long ago in Italy. Francis used real people to tell the story of the shepherds, angels, and three kings coming to see the Holy Family. Then people began to make small wooden statues to put under their trees at home.

Children around the world put pieces of straw in empty cribs each time they do a good deed. This tradition began in France. On Christmas the crib is filled with straw to keep Jesus warm in his bed.

In Africa, drums are used to announce important events. On Christmas Day the sound of drums can be heard in churches and neighborhoods. Later, neighbors eat a special meal. Every family brings a dish to share. The families sing and dance to welcome Jesus.

Christmas traditions help people all over the world celebrate Jesus' birth. Traditions help us remember that Jesus is "Joy to the World!"

Activity

How does your family celebrate Christmas? Write one or two of your family traditions on the lines below.

Christmas Morning

On Christmas morning, Michael and his family were awake early. They opened gifts and sang songs. They called Nana and Granddad to say "Merry Christmas!" Then everyone hurried to get ready for Mass.

The church was very beautiful. Michael liked the poinsettia plants around the altar. Michael's father told a story about the flower. He called it the "flower of the holy night."

Father Bowman wore white vestments. He began Mass by saying, "Today our Savior is born! Joy to the world!"

After Mass, Michael's family knelt in front of the Christmas stable. They prayed and thanked God for Jesus.

Activity

Unscramble the letters on each flower to form a word. Then use the words to complete the prayer. Pray the prayer aloud together.

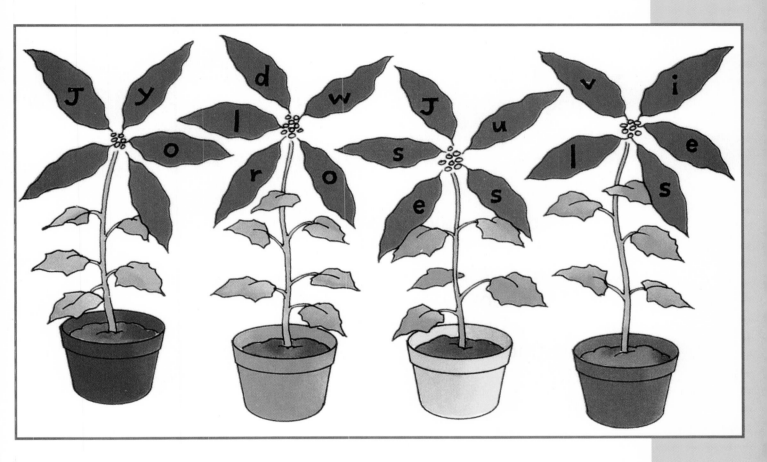

_____   _____

_____ to the _____!

_____ has come into our

_____. Alleluia!

A Christmas Project

Make a Christmas story box for your room. Follow the directions given by your teacher to make your story box. These are the things you will need.

- construction paper
- craft sticks
- string
- glue
- crayons
- scissors

Think about a picture to draw on your box. You can draw Mary, Joseph, and Jesus in the stable. You can draw shepherds in the field. You can draw a picture of your family on Christmas.

Write a Christmas message on the back of the box.

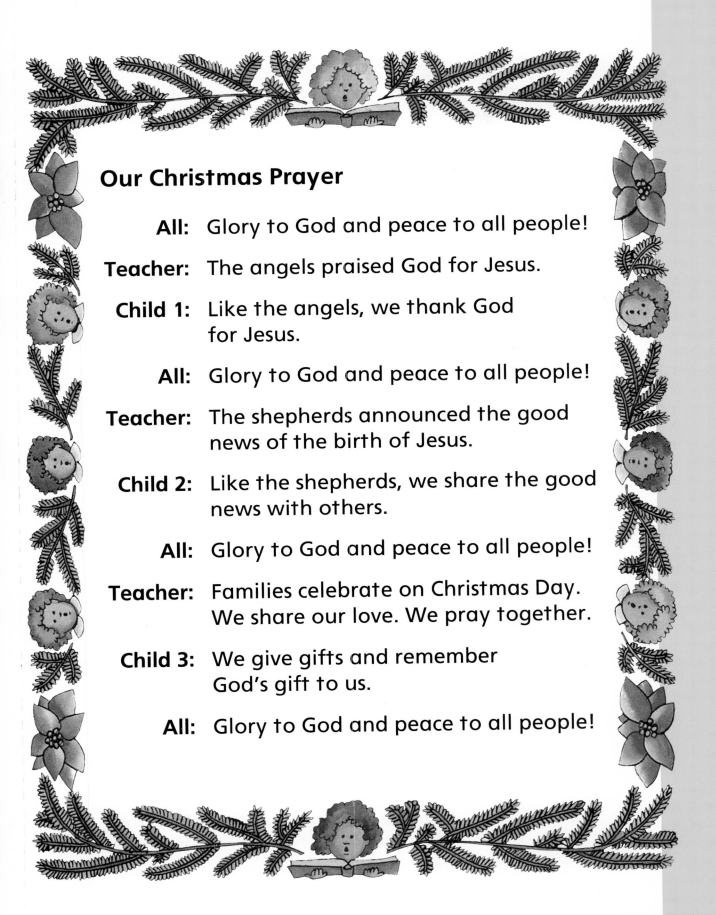

Our Christmas Prayer

All: Glory to God and peace to all people!

Teacher: The angels praised God for Jesus.

Child 1: Like the angels, we thank God for Jesus.

All: Glory to God and peace to all people!

Teacher: The shepherds announced the good news of the birth of Jesus.

Child 2: Like the shepherds, we share the good news with others.

All: Glory to God and peace to all people!

Teacher: Families celebrate on Christmas Day. We share our love. We pray together.

Child 3: We give gifts and remember God's gift to us.

All: Glory to God and peace to all people!

Our Church Celebrates Lent

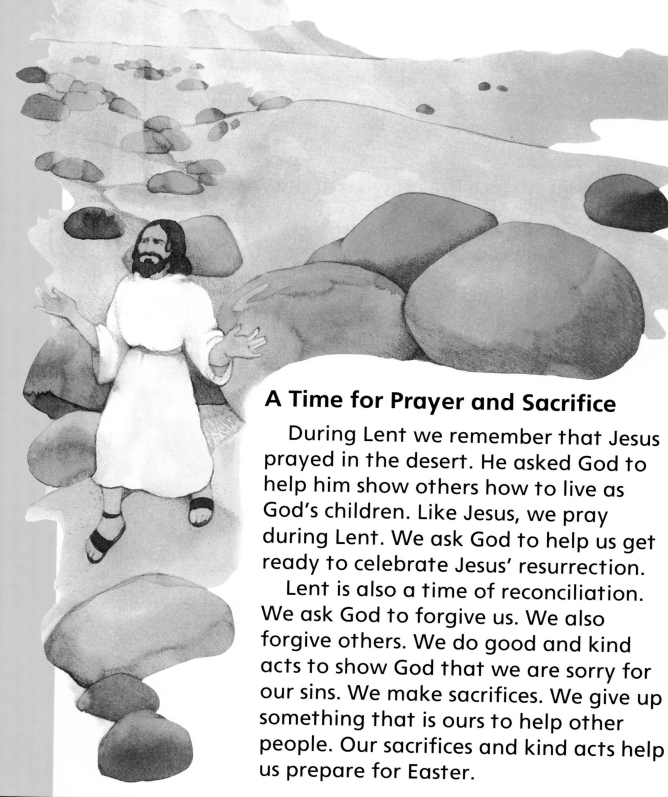

A Time for Prayer and Sacrifice

During Lent we remember that Jesus prayed in the desert. He asked God to help him show others how to live as God's children. Like Jesus, we pray during Lent. We ask God to help us get ready to celebrate Jesus' resurrection.

Lent is also a time of reconciliation. We ask God to forgive us. We also forgive others. We do good and kind acts to show God that we are sorry for our sins. We make sacrifices. We give up something that is ours to help other people. Our sacrifices and kind acts help us prepare for Easter.

Activity

Find your way through the maze to Jesus. There are letters along the way. As you come to each letter, copy it on the line below. The letters will form a word to complete the sentence.

During Lent, God is pleased by our

_____

- -

_____ .

Preparing for Easter

Sister Joan's class was talking about Lent. Sister wrote the word **sacrifice** on the board. She told the children that to sacrifice means to give something out of love. Making sacrifices helps us prepare for Easter.

"How can we sacrifice during Lent?" Sister Joan asked.

"I will give up dessert for Lent," said Hal.

"I will let my brother watch his favorite TV show," said Lisa.

The other children thought of sacrifices they could make. They prayed together, asking God to help them make the sacrifices they had chosen.

Activity

Circle the word hidden in each line. The words tell how we can sacrifice during Lent.

G	I	V	E	J	E	S
S	H	A	R	E	T	H
K	L	O	V	E	D	A
I	P	R	A	Y	L	O
E	C	A	R	E	G	N

Finish this letter about a sacrifice you will make to get ready for Easter.

Dear Jesus, _____

_____

During Lent, I will _____

_____

_____

_____

_____

_____

_____ .

Love,

_____

_____

The Church Prays During Lent

Our Church has special ways of praying during the forty days of Lent. These prayers help us remember that Lent is a time to change. When we pray, we think about how we have been living. We ask God to help us be more like Jesus.

Ash Wednesday is the first day of Lent. When we go to church, the priest or another minister traces the sign of the cross on our foreheads with ashes. The ashes are a sign that we want to follow Jesus more closely.

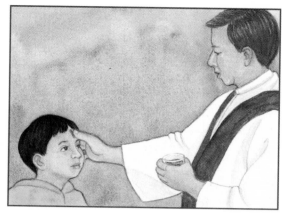

During Lent we can pray the Stations of the Cross with our class or families. The Stations of the Cross tell us how Jesus died. In church we see pictures or statues that show Jesus going to Calvary, the place where he died. We call each picture a station—a place where we stop to pray. At each station we remember how Jesus showed his love for us.

Lent is also a time to celebrate the sacrament of Reconciliation. We think about the times we haven't acted with love. We tell God we are sorry for our sins. We ask God to help us grow in love so that we can share in Jesus' new life on Easter.

Activity

Solve this coded message. The message is a prayer that the Church prays during Lent. Copy each letter on the spaces below. As you do this, follow these directions.

- Change every A to E.
- Change every E to A.
- Change every O to U.
- Change every U to O.
- Change every S to T.
- Change every T to S.

DAER JATOT,
HALP OT SORN EWEY FRUM TIN. HALP OT SU LIVA
SHA GUUD NAWT.

_____ _____,

_____ __ ____ ____ __ ____ ___.

____ __ __ __ ____ __ ____ _____.

A Time for Fasting

Fasting is one way we can sacrifice during Lent. Fasting is eating less food than we usually do. During Lent the Church asks grown-ups to fast in a special way.

Children can fast during Lent, too. We can decide not to eat between meals. We can give up candy or another treat. We may choose not to eat dessert for the forty days of Lent. God does not want us to stop eating healthy meals during Lent. God always wants us to keep our bodies strong.

Long ago, people fasted during Lent by not eating anything made with eggs, yeast, butter, or milk. Bread is made with all these ingredients, so the people did not eat regular bread. They made a special Lenten bread with flour, water, and salt. They twisted the bread into the shape of two arms crossed in prayer. Today, we call this special Lenten bread pretzels.

At meals during Lent we can eat pretzels. It will remind us that Lent is a time to pray and fast.

A Prayer for Lent

Dear God,
Please accept our sacrifices during Lent.
Help us to follow Jesus always.
Amen.

Activity

How will you fast during Lent?
On the pretzel, write the name of a favorite food
or activity that you will give up during Lent.

A Lenten Project

This cross will help you get ready for Easter. Make a sacrifice each day. Find ways to do good and kind things for others.

Number all the squares. Each day that you make a sacrifice, color a square.

Our Prayer for Lent

Group 1: Lent is a time to pray.
Be with us, O God, as we pray.

Group 2: Lent is a time of reconciliation.
Forgive us, O God, and give us
forgiving hearts.

Group 1: Lent is a time of sacrifice.
Help us, O God, to be kind and good
to others.

Group 2: Lent is a time to prepare for Easter.
Make us ready, O God, for the resurrection
of Jesus.

Teacher: The Lord says, "I will give you a new heart.
I will put my spirit within you."

Based on Ezekiel 36:26–27

All: We pray,
Give us a new heart, O God!
Put your Spirit within us!

Our Church Celebrates Holy Week

Three Special Days of Prayer

We celebrate the three holiest days of the year when Lent ends. They begin on Holy Thursday evening and end on Easter Sunday evening.

On Holy Thursday night we remember Jesus' Last Supper. During Mass, the priest washes the feet of twelve people. This is what Jesus did the night before he died. The washing of feet reminds us to serve others.

On Good Friday we go to church to hear the story of Jesus' death on the cross. We show our love for Jesus by kissing a special cross or by touching it with our hands. Then we all pray The Lord's Prayer together and receive Jesus in the Eucharist.

On Holy Saturday and Easter Sunday we remember that Jesus died to give us new life.

On Holy Saturday night the Easter candle is lighted. It shows that Jesus has risen. We hold lighted candles. They are a sign of our Baptism, when Jesus gave us new life. We welcome new members to our Church. We celebrate with joy.

During these three holy days, we pray, "Jesus, our Light. Thanks be to God!" (based on The Easter Vigil Procession, *Sacramentary*).

Activity

Draw lines to match the three most holy days to their pictures.

Holy Thursday

Good Friday

Holy Saturday evening

Holy Thursday

The week before Easter is Holy Week. It is a special time in the Church. We remember the words and actions of Jesus from the days before he rose from the dead. At Mass on Holy Thursday, we remember the Last Supper, the special meal Jesus shared with his friends.

During Mass the bread and wine become Jesus' body and blood. The priest reminds us that Jesus gave himself to us in the Eucharist.

On Holy Thursday we remember Jesus by celebrating the Eucharist. We thank Jesus for giving us the gift of himself.

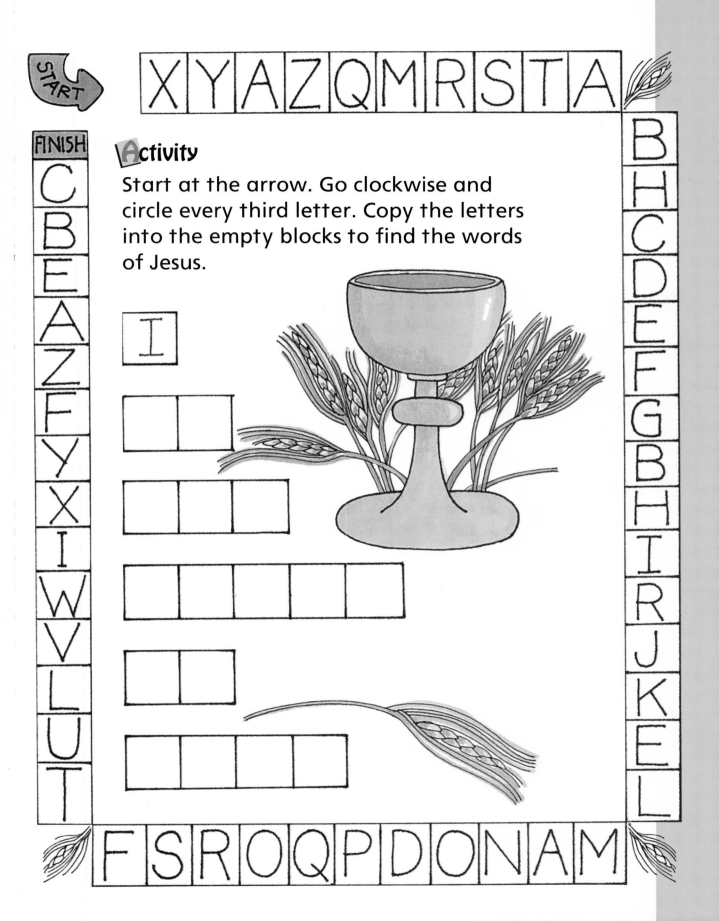

START

FINISH

Activity

Start at the arrow. Go clockwise and circle every third letter. Copy the letters into the empty blocks to find the words of Jesus.

X Y A Z Q M R S T A

B H C D E F G B H I R J K E L

C B E A Z F Y X I W V L U T

F S R O Q P D O N A M

I

Our Church Celebrates Easter

Jesus Is Risen

Early on Sunday morning, when it was still dark, Mary of Magdala went to Jesus' tomb. Mary was a friend and follower of Jesus. When Mary got to the

tomb, she saw that the stone in front of it had been rolled away. She went to tell Jesus' followers.

Mary said, "They have taken Jesus' body away from the tomb. I don't know where they have put him."

Peter and a friend ran to the tomb. His friend ran faster than Peter. When they got to the tomb, they looked inside. Peter went into the tomb. He saw the cloths that had been used to wrap Jesus' body. Then Peter's friend went into the tomb. He too saw the cloths in which Jesus had been buried. He saw them and believed that Jesus had risen from the dead.

Later that day, Jesus appeared to his followers. He praised them for believing that he had risen. He said, "Blessed are you who believed."

(Based on John 20:1-9, 29)

On Easter we celebrate Jesus' new life. We remember that Jesus rose from the dead. Jesus promises us that we will share in his new life. Like Peter's friend, we believe in Jesus' promise to us.

Activity

Follow the path from the empty tomb to the risen Jesus. Copy the letters you find along the way to complete the Easter prayer.

We pray, " _____ Jesus is risen!"

A Time of Great Happiness

One morning after Jesus had risen, his friends were fishing. Suddenly they saw Jesus standing on the beach. They brought their boat to shore so that they could visit with their friend.

Jesus had made a fire. He told his friends to bring some of the fish they had caught to cook for breakfast. Jesus shared cooked fish and bread with his friends.

They were excited. This was the third time that Jesus visited them after he rose to new life.

Based on John 21:8–14

Celebrating Jesus' New Life

In the weeks following Easter Sunday, we continue to celebrate Jesus' resurrection. At Mass we gather with the parish community to remember what Jesus did for us. We celebrate his rising to new life. By sharing the Eucharist we remember that Jesus is always with us.

Activity

Unscramble the letters on each fish to form a word. Then use the words to complete the prayer.

_____

We praise you, _____

_____   _____

_____ of _____.

Waiting for a Letter

Beth watched for the mail carrier every day. Beth was waiting for a letter from her best friend, Meg. Two weeks ago, Meg and her family had moved to another town. Beth missed Meg. She felt sad and alone.

Each day Debby gave Beth the mail. "No letter today, Beth," she said.

Beth kept hoping to hear from Meg. One day Debby took a letter from her pouch and asked, "Is this what you have been waiting for?"

Beth quickly opened the letter. It was from Meg. Beth smiled and said, "Meg did not forget me!" Then she went to share the news with her family.

Activity

Meg did not forget Beth. Like Meg, Jesus will not forget us. Jesus said, "I am with you always."

Choose a word from the box to complete each sentence.

1. Jesus is with us in the sacrament of the

_____

- -

_____.

2. Jesus is with us in the

_____

- -

_____.

3. Jesus is with us in other

_____

- -

_____.

An Easter Project

Follow the directions your teacher gives you to make a tissue paper Easter egg card. These are the things you will need.

- paper
- scissors
- glue
- tissue paper
- pencil

This is what you will do.

1. Fold a sheet of paper in half.

2. Cut a double egg out of the paper.

3. Cut shapes out of the cover of the card.

4. Glue pieces of tissue paper over the cutouts on the cover.

5. Write an Easter message inside the card.

Our Easter Prayer

Jesus died for us.
Alleluia!
Jesus is risen to new life.
Alleluia!
Jesus is always with us.
Alleluia!

Jesus,
teach us to know you better by doing good
for others. Help us grow in your love and
understand your new life.
Amen.

Based on the Opening Prayer
for Saturday, the Sixth Week
of Easter

Our Church Honors Saints

Mother Frances Cabrini

When Frances Cabrini was a little girl in Italy, she planned to help people. When Frances got older, she became a teacher.

One day a priest asked her to take care of children who did not have parents. Frances began her work by caring for the children. Soon Frances asked other women to help her with her work. People began to call her Mother Cabrini.

Then Mother Cabrini was asked to go to the United States. She knew God was calling her to do special work. With the help of many people, she built schools and hospitals. She never got tired of helping people.

We honor Mother Cabrini on November 13. We pray, "God, help us live good lives. Help us to do your work."

Activity

Think about what work you want to do when you are older. Draw a picture of yourself doing that work.

John the Baptizer

When John the Baptizer was a young man, he went into the desert. He wanted to discover God's plan for him. He prayed and fasted. God told him what to do.

John baptized many people. He told them, "Someone is coming who will baptize you with the Holy Spirit."

Jesus came to John to be baptized. Then Jesus began to do God's work in the world. He healed people. He brought them God's love and forgiveness.

Jesus said that no man was greater than John. People who follow Jesus can learn even more about God's love than John knew.

Based on Matthew 3:1–17, 11:4–11

Activity

We honor the birth of Saint John the Baptizer on June 24. This prayer can help us to be like Saint John.

Unscramble the letters below each line. Then fill in the words to complete the prayer.

_____ _____

_____ us _____ others

elHp · lelt

_____ _____

about _____. Help us _____

seJus · od

_____ _____

God's _____ in the _____.

korw · orldw

Saint Angela

Angela learned about God from her parents. They told Angela many stories about God and Jesus. They taught her to pray every day.

When Angela was ten years old, her parents died. Angela went to live with her uncle. Angela grew closer to God every day. She wanted others to know about God's goodness and love.

When Angela grew up, she saw that many children were not learning how to follow Jesus. She began to tell the children the same stories her parents had told her.

Other women joined Angela. With Angela as their leader, they began schools for poor children. These women became known as the Ursuline sisters.

We honor Saint Angela on January 27 as a great teacher and leader. Like Saint Angela, we can pray, "Help us know and love you, O God!"

Activity

Print the name of your Catholic school on the banner below. Then in the cloud, write one thing you have learned about God or Jesus in your Catholic school.

Saint John Bosco

The boys from the village watched the young man do magic tricks. They laughed and clapped and asked for more. Then the man took the boys to Mass. He taught them about Jesus.

The man was John Bosco, a priest who cared for poor boys. Some of the boys had no homes of their own. John Bosco asked rich people for money so that he could build a school and make a home for the boys.

John Bosco treated the children with love and kindness. He knew that children learned best when they could have fun. He taught the boys to love God. He taught them how to sew clothes and make shoes. When the boys grew up, they were able to find work because of all that John Bosco had taught them.

We remember Saint John Bosco on his feast day, January 31.

We Pray to the Saints

Child 1: Mother Frances Cabrini, you are our example of caring.

All: Teach us, Mother Frances Cabrini.

Child 2: Saint John the Baptizer, you are our example of how to follow God's word.

All: Teach us, Saint John the Baptizer.

Child 3: Saint John Bosco, you are our example of joy and trust in God.

All: Teach us, Saint John Bosco.

All: We can follow, we can follow.
We can trust, we can trust.
We listen to God's word.
We listen to God's word.
We can share, we can share.

Our Church Honors Mary

The Visitation

One day, Mary went to visit her cousin, Elizabeth. When Elizabeth saw Mary coming, she ran out to meet her.

"Hail, Mary!" Elizabeth said. "Blessed are you among women." Elizabeth was telling Mary how very special she was to be the mother of God's Son, Jesus.

Mary thought about what Elizabeth said to her. Mary was so happy to be Jesus' mother that she began to thank and praise God.

Based on Luke 1:39–45

Thanking God for Jesus

Every year on May 31, the Church remembers Mary's visit to Elizabeth. We call this day the Feast of the Visitation. On this day we, like Mary, thank and praise God for the gift of Jesus.

Activity

Think about all the things God has done for you. Below, write a prayer of thanks and praise to God. Share your prayer with your family and friends.

My Prayer

The Wedding at Cana

Jesus and his friends went to a wedding in the town called Cana. Mary, the mother of Jesus, was also there. At the wedding, Mary and Jesus spent time together. They talked and visited.

Mary saw that the wedding party had run out of wine. She saw that the people who were giving the party were embarrassed. Mary was worried that the guests would leave. She wanted people to stay and celebrate the wedding.

Mary asked Jesus to help. Jesus wanted to please his mother. He knew how much she cared about other people. So Jesus asked the servants to fill stone jars with water. When the servants poured from the jars, the water had become fine wine.

Based on John 2:1–9

Find your way through the maze to Mary and Jesus.
Use the words in the maze to complete the sentence
below. Then write how you can show care for
another person.

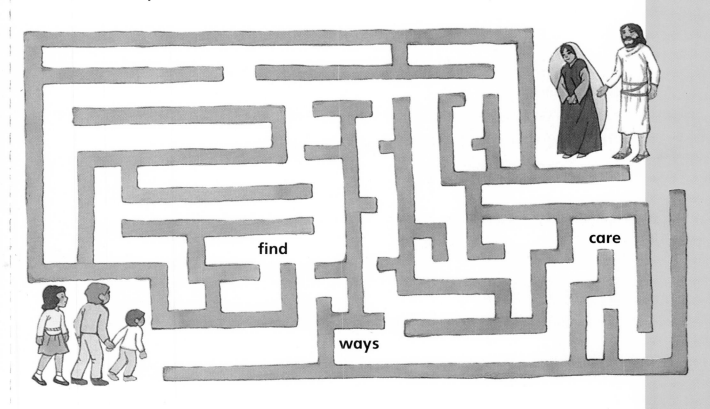

Mary and Jesus help us learn to _____

_____ _____

_____ to _____ for others.

I can show care for _____

_____

by _____

The Rosary

The Rosary is a special prayer that honors Mary. When we pray the Rosary, we remember Jesus' and Mary's lives. We remember that Mary was Jesus' mother. We remember that Mary always said yes to God.

We can pray the Rosary alone. We can pray it together in school, at home, or in church. We can pray the Rosary silently or aloud. Mary always brings our prayers to Jesus. When we pray the Rosary, we ask Mary, "Pray for us that we may love and follow Jesus, your son."

Praying the Rosary

When we pray a decade of the Rosary, we think about an important time in Mary's and Jesus' lives. We call these important times **mysteries**. The mysteries are the special things that God has done for us through Jesus and Mary.

Activity

Pray a decade of the Rosary each day this week with your class or family. When you have finished praying the Rosary, draw your own rosary in the space below.

Our Church Celebrates Holy Days

The Feast of Corpus Christi

The words <u>Corpus Christi</u> are Latin words that mean "the body of Christ." On the Feast of Corpus Christi, now called the Feast of the Body and Blood of Christ, we think about the Eucharist. We thank Jesus for the gift of himself.

In some parishes, people thank Jesus by having a procession. As they walk, they pray and honor the presence of Jesus in the Eucharist.

We celebrate the Feast of Corpus Christi on a Sunday that falls nine weeks after Easter. On this day we remember the words of Jesus.

"I am the living bread. Anyone who eats this bread will live forever."

Based on John 6:51

Activity

Use this code to color the stained-glass window.

1 yellow   **3** green   **5** blue

2 brown   **4** purple

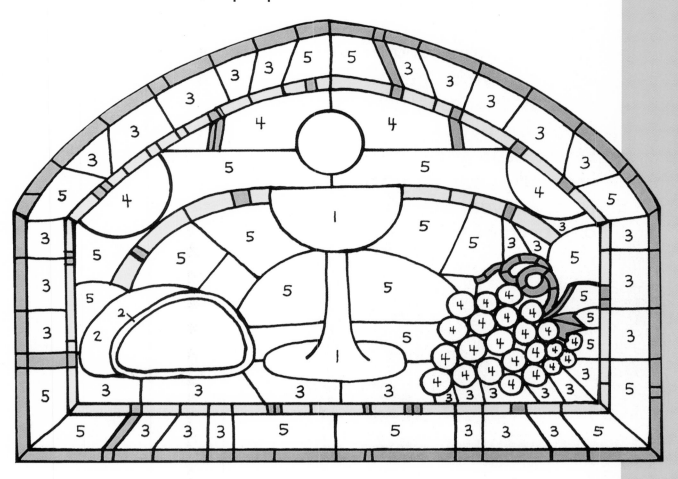

On the lines below, write a short prayer to Jesus.

The Coming of the Holy Spirit

All of Jesus' friends were together. Suddenly they heard a loud noise that sounded like the wind. The sound filled the whole house. They saw flames of fire around them. All of Jesus' friends were filled with the Holy Spirit. They began to praise and thank God in many different languages.

Jesus' friends left the house and began to teach the people in the streets about Jesus, the Savior, who had risen to new life. Many people listened and believed in what Jesus' friends taught. Every day, new people were baptized and became followers of Jesus.

Based on the Acts of the Apostles 2:1–41

Pentecost

After Jesus rose to new life, he returned to God in heaven. He knew his followers would need help sharing the good news. Jesus promised that he would send the Holy Spirit.

The Holy Spirit came on **Pentecost**. We celebrate Pentecost fifty days after Easter. Pentecost is the birthday of the Church.

On Pentecost we pray, "Come, Holy Spirit, let your love shine brightly in us."

Activity

Find the word in the box that completes each sentence. Then put the story of Pentecost in order by numbering each sentence. Use the numbers 1 through 6.

teach	fire	Jesus'	baptized	wind	Holy Spirit

◯ They heard a sound like __ __ __ __.

◯ They were filled with the __ __ __ __ __ __ __ __ __ __.

◯ All of __ __ __ __ __ friends were together.

◯ Every day new people were __ __ __ __ __ __ __ __.

◯ They saw flames of __ __ __ __.

◯ They began to __ __ __ __ __ the people about Jesus.

Thanksgiving

Long ago the Pilgrims invited their Native American friends to a feast. These Native Americans had given them seeds to plant. They had taught the Pilgrims how to hunt and grow food. The Pilgrims thanked the Native Americans for helping them learn how to live in America. The friends celebrated together. Soon the celebration became known as Thanksgiving Day.

On Thanksgiving we think about all the good things that God gives us. We eat special foods. We celebrate with our families. We remember that some people are hungry. Like the Pilgrims, we share our food. Like the Native Americans, we welcome strangers to our land, churches, and homes.

On Thanksgiving Day we pray, "God, you are great and good. Your love lasts forever" (based on Psalm 100:5).

A Thanksgiving Picture-Story Prayer

Thank you, God, for making me.

Thank you for my  .

Thank you for the and  ,

for and and that fly.

Thank you for the  we eat,

for and and fields of  .

Thank you for a that mends,

for , our , and special  .

Thank you most for , who sets us free.

O God, we praise you always, thankfully.

In the Spirit of Jesus

Pope John XXIII

Angelo Joseph Roncalli was a very good man. After he became a priest, he worked in a school. He also worked in the army, teaching the soldiers about Jesus.

He also taught them about the Catholic Church.

Father Angelo Roncalli became a leader in the Church. When he was a bishop, he cared for many people. He helped those who were in trouble. He invited many people without families into his home. Bishop Roncalli tried to lead others to Jesus.

After many years, Bishop Roncalli was chosen to be pope, the leader of the Roman Catholic Church. He chose the name Pope John XXIII (the twenty-third). As a world leader he talked to all people about peace. He wanted everyone to work together. He knew that when people love others, Jesus lives in their hearts.

 Activity

Look at the picture. Write your answers to the
questions below. Then color the picture.

1. What is happening in the picture?

_____

- -

_____

- -

_____

2. How can you be like Pope John XXIII?

_____

- -

_____

- -

_____

A Visit from Father Jim

"Boys and girls," said Sister Joan. "We have a special visitor today. Father Jim is a Maryknoll priest. He is going to tell us about his work."

"Hello, children," said Father Jim. "Does anyone know what a **missionary** is?"

Corey said, "A missionary tells people about God."

"That's right!" said Father. "A missionary travels to faraway lands to share the good news about God and Jesus."

"Where do you go?" asked Jorge.

"Maryknoll priests and sisters go all over the world," said Father Jim. He showed the children a globe. He pointed to the places he had gone. He showed them Africa, Central America, and South America.

"What do you do there?" asked Alexa.

"Maryknoll priests and sisters live with the people. We teach them to pray. We talk about God. We build churches and schools," said Father Jim. "We believe that everyone has the right to hear about Jesus."

Activity

Follow Father Jim's journey from continent to continent. Unscramble the letters on each continent to form a word. Use the words to complete the sentence at the bottom of the page.

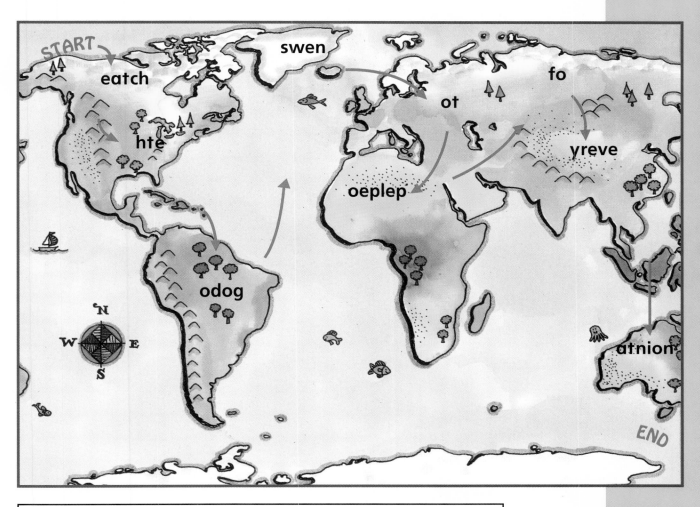

Jesus says,

"____ ____ ____ ____ ____ ____ ____

____ ____ ____ ____ ____ ____ ____

____ ____ ____ ____ ____ ____ ____ . "

OUR CATHOLIC HERITAGE

What Catholics Believe

Catholic Christians share many special gifts. We believe, live, and pray as one family.

ABOUT the Bible

The Bible is a book that is special to many people who believe in God. The book is divided into two parts: the Old and the New Testaments. The Old Testament includes many stories of God's people who lived before Jesus was born.

The New Testament is the second part of the Bible. The Holy Spirit helped some followers of Jesus write the books and letters in this section. Four of the books are the Gospels of Matthew, Mark, Luke, and John. In these books, the gospel writers wrote about the wonderful things that Jesus said and did. The gospel writers also tell us about the places where Jesus lived and visited.

The Gospel of Matthew tells about the birth of Jesus in Bethlehem. The Gospel of Mark tells about the baptism of Jesus in the River Jordan. The Gospel of Luke tells us that Jesus, Mary, and Joseph lived in Nazareth. The Gospel of John tells about the Last Supper in Jerusalem.

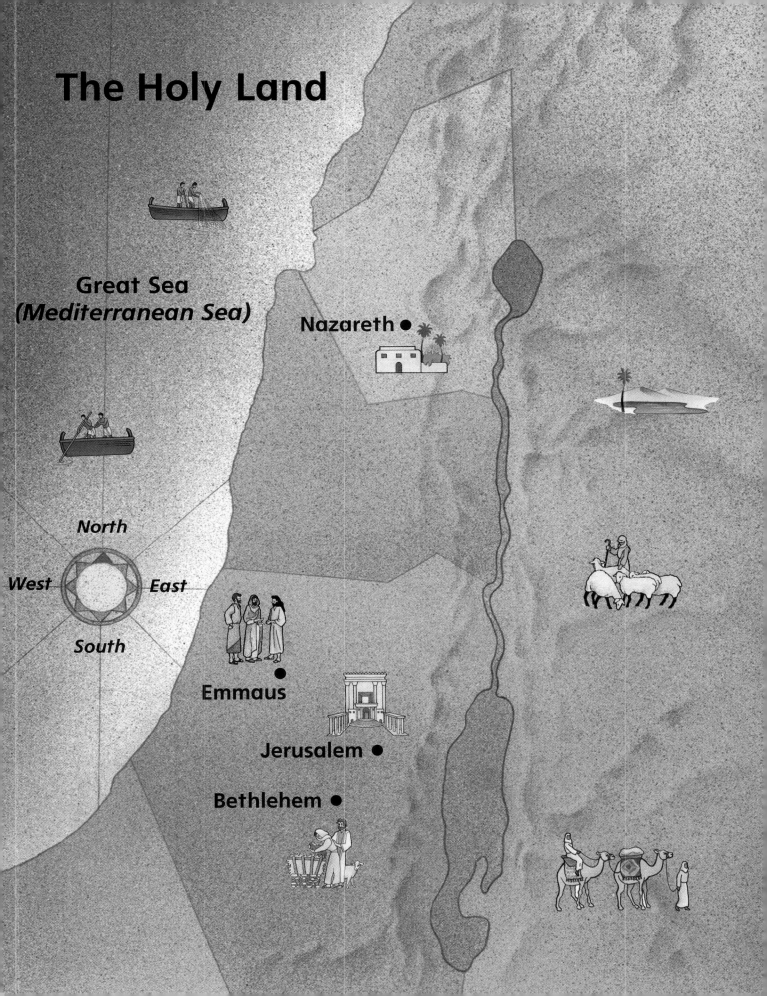

The Holy Land

Great Sea
(Mediterranean Sea)

Nazareth ●

North

West   East

South

Emmaus ●

Jerusalem ●

Bethlehem ●

ABOUT the Trinity

We Believe in God

There is only one God. God is three persons: Father, Son, and Holy Spirit.

God is our Creator. God made all things with love. Everything God made is good.

The Bible is a special book about God's love for us. God speaks to us in the Bible.

We share in God's life. **Grace** is God's life and love in us.

God loves and cares for us. God wants us to be happy. God gives us Jesus to help us.

We Believe in Jesus

Jesus is God's Son, who became a man and lived on earth with us. God sent Jesus to show us how to love.

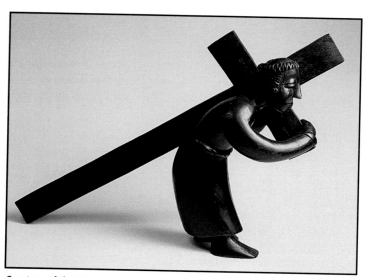

Courtesy of the S.M.A. Fathers

Jesus is our brother and friend. Jesus is our teacher. Jesus teaches us how to live as children of God.

Jesus died on the cross and rose from the dead for us. Jesus is our **Savior**. He saves us from sin and death.

Jesus is always with us. Jesus shares his new life with us.

We Believe in the Holy Spirit

The Holy Spirit is the Spirit of God. God's Spirit helps us follow Jesus.

We receive the Holy Spirit at Baptism. The Spirit of God gives us gifts to help us live good lives. The Holy Spirit helps us to be **holy**. To be holy means to be like God.

ABOUT the Catholic Church

We are **Catholic Christians**. We follow Jesus. We belong to the Catholic Church. We celebrate the sacraments. We pray to God, and we help others.

The pope is the leader of the Catholic Church. We call the pope our Holy Father.

The Church is the people of God. We help God's love grow in the world.

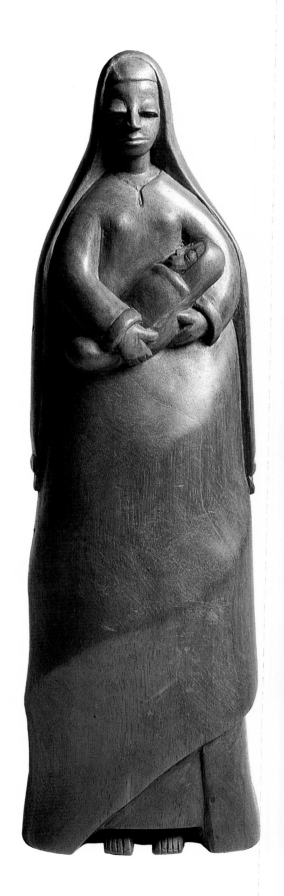

ABOUT Mary

God chose Mary to be Jesus' mother. Mary loved and trusted God. From the first moment of life, Mary was filled with grace.

Mary is our mother, too. Mary loves and cares for us.

Mary is our greatest **saint**. The **saints** are special people who show us how to follow Jesus. We honor the saints and ask them to pray for us.

ABOUT New Life Forever

Jesus teaches us that if we act with love, we will live forever. We will be happy with God in **heaven**. Heaven is unending happiness with God and all who love God. If we show love for God and others, we will be happy together in heaven.

❀ How Catholics Worship

Worship is giving honor and praise to God. We worship God in the sacraments and prayer.

ABOUT the Sacraments

The **sacraments** are celebrations of God's love and signs of Jesus' presence with us now. There are seven sacraments.

Baptism is a sacrament of welcome into the Church. At Baptism we receive the Holy Spirit.

We are baptized with water. Water is a sign that we share Jesus' new life.

In the sacrament of Confirmation, we receive the Holy Spirit in a special way. God's Spirit helps us to tell everyone the good news about Jesus.

At Mass, we share a special meal with Jesus. The **sacrament of the Eucharist** celebrates the presence of Jesus in the Eucharist we share.

At Mass, we remember that Jesus died on the cross for us. At Mass, we thank God for giving us Jesus, the Bread of Life.

In the **sacrament of Reconciliation,** we say we are sorry for our sins. We celebrate God's forgiveness.

Anointing of the Sick brings Jesus' peace and help to people who are sick or elderly.

In the sacrament of **Holy Orders**, men become priests and join Jesus' work in a special way.

The **sacrament of Matrimony** celebrates the love of a man and a woman for each other.

ABOUT the Mass

1. Our celebration begins. The priest and other ministers walk down the aisle in a procession. We stand and sing a gathering song.

2. The priest welcomes us. He says "The Lord be with you." We answer, "And also with you." We all make the sign of the cross.

3. We remember our sins and God's love and forgiveness. The priest prays an opening prayer.

4. We listen to God's word in readings from the Old Testament and the New Testament.

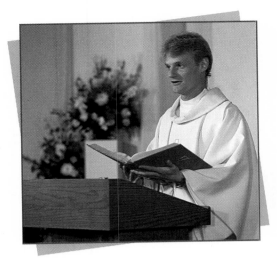

5. In the gospel story, we hear about Jesus' life and teachings. We stand to welcome Jesus in the gospel.

6. The priest or deacon explains the readings to us in a special talk called a homily.

7. We pray for the Church, for our country, and for all God's people. We call this prayer the Prayer of the Faithful.

8. We prepare the altar for the meal we are about to share. We bring our gifts of bread and wine. Sometimes we bring other gifts, too. We always bring ourselves, the most important gift of all.

9. The priest offers our gifts of bread and wine to God. They will become the body and blood of Jesus.

10. We thank and praise God for all God's blessings, especially for the gift of Jesus.

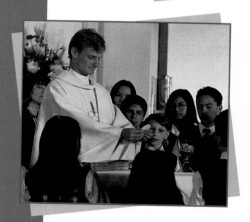

11. Our gifts of bread and wine become for us the body and blood of Jesus. We call the body and blood of Jesus <u>Eucharist</u>.

12. The priest holds up the Eucharist and prays a prayer of praise to God. We answer, "Amen!" Amen means, "Yes! We believe this is true."

13. We pray together The Lord's Prayer, the prayer that Jesus taught us.

14. We offer one another a sign of peace to show that we are all brothers and sisters in Jesus.

15. We come to the table of the Lord to receive Jesus in the Eucharist.

16. We receive God's blessing and say, "Amen." We sing a song of praise. Then we go in peace to love and serve all people.

ABOUT Reconciliation

The sacrament of Reconciliation celebrates God's love and forgiveness. Sometimes we celebrate the sacrament of Reconciliation with the Catholic community.

Opening Song   We sing a song of praise.

Greeting and Opening Prayer   The priest welcomes us and prays with us.

Readings and Gospel   We listen to stories from the Bible.

Homily   The priest or deacon explains God's word to us.

Examination of Conscience   We think about our words and actions. Together we pray The Lord's Prayer.

General Confession of Sins   We pray a prayer of sorrow.

Individual Confession   Now we are ready to go one by one to the priest. We talk about the words and actions for which we are sorry. We ask forgiveness. We receive absolution.

Prayer of Thanksgiving   We praise and thank God for God's mercy.

Blessing and Dismissal   The priest asks God's blessing on us. We sing a song of praise.

I say a prayer of contrition.

A Prayer of Sorrow

My God,
I am sorry for my sins
with all my heart.

In choosing to do wrong
and failing to do good,
I have sinned against you
whom I should love
above all things.

I firmly intend, with your
help, to do penance,
to sin no more, and to avoid
whatever leads me to sin.

Rite of Penance

6

Fold

The priest reads a story from
the Bible.

The story reminds me that God is
always ready to forgive me.

3

The priest says, **Go in peace.**
I answer, **Amen.**

The priest and I thank God
for being forgiving.

8

MY RECONCILIATION
BOOK

Name

I

I confess my sins.

The priest listens as I talk about how I have turned away from God and hurt myself or others.

4

The priest gives me a penance.

The priest asks me to say a prayer or do a good act. This will show God that I am sorry and want to be more caring.

5

I examine my conscience.

I think about things I have said or done to hurt God, other people or myself.

2

The priest gives me absolution.

The priest says,
I absolve you from your sins in the name of the Father, and of the Son, and of the Holy Spirit.

7

When we receive Communion, the priest or special minister says,

The body of Christ.

We respond, **Amen.**

fold

The priest shows us the chalice.

He says,
**Take this, all of you, and drink from it:
this is the cup of my blood,
the blood of the new and everlasting
   covenant.
It will be shed for you and for all
so that sins may be forgiven.
Do this in memory of me.**

After Communion, we thank Jesus. We can say this prayer.

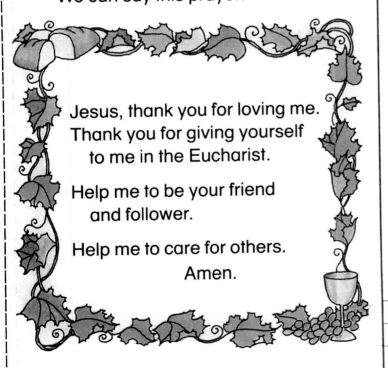

Jesus, thank you for loving me.
Thank you for giving yourself
   to me in the Eucharist.

Help me to be your friend
   and follower.

Help me to care for others.
          Amen.

MY COMMUNION BOOK

Name

Then the priest says,
**Let us proclaim the mystery
of faith.**

We respond,
   **Christ has died,
   Christ is risen,
   Christ will come again.**

4

Before we receive Communion,
the priest says,
**This is the Lamb of God
who takes away the sins of the world.
Happy are those who are called
   to his supper.**

We respond,
**Lord, I am not worthy to receive you,
but only say the word and
I shall be healed.**

5

At Mass we remember Jesus'
words and actions at the Last
Supper. The priest shows
us the bread.

He says,
**Take this, all of you, and eat it:
this is my body which will be
   given up for you.**

2

If we receive from the cup,
the priest or special minister
says,
   The blood of Christ.

We respond, **Amen.**

7

✿ How Catholics Live

Jesus teaches us how to live. The Holy Spirit and the Church help us live with love.

The Great Commandment

Jesus said, "Love God with all your heart, all your thoughts, and all your strength. Love your neighbor as yourself" (based on Mark 12:31).

Jesus teaches us to live the **Great Commandment**. The Great Commandment tells us how to show our love for God and our neighbor.

ABOUT the Commandments

We can find God's commandments in the Bible. God gave us the Ten Commandments to help us live the way God wants us to live.

We Live God's Laws	
We show our love for God.	We believe in God and love God.
	We use God's name with love.
	We pray to God every day.
	We pray with our Church family at Mass on Sunday.
We show our love for our neighbor.	We obey our parents and those who care for us.
	We care for all living things.
	We tell the truth.
	We are careful with other people's things.
	We share with others.
	We are thankful for God's gifts.

Jesus' New Commandment

Jesus gave us a new commandment. He said, "Love one another as I love you" (based on John 15:12).

We can love like Jesus by being fair and kind. We can help others. We can be peacemakers.

When we do not act with love, we **sin**. Sin is choosing to do what we know is wrong.

The Holy Spirit Helps Us

We can choose to love. We can choose to sin. The Holy Spirit helps us choose to do what is good and to turn away from sin.

ABOUT Vocations

When we were baptized, we began our new life as Catholic Christians. As we grow older, we know that we will be invited by God to live more and more as Jesus taught us. God calls each person to help others in a special way. This is called our **vocation**.

Many Ways of Helping

Most Catholics are called by God to help others as members of their parish church. They can help at Mass by reading the Scriptures, leading the songs, giving Eucharist, or by helping in other ways. They can teach others about God and Jesus' message found in the gospels. They can do many things to help others.

Sometimes God calls people to a special way of helping in the Church. There are priests who lead the parish community. There are religious brothers and sisters who teach, serve the poor, or help lead the parish. There are deacons who help in the parish by reading the gospel at Mass or by giving the homily. Deacons help in many other ways, too.

▲ A priest visits a classroom.

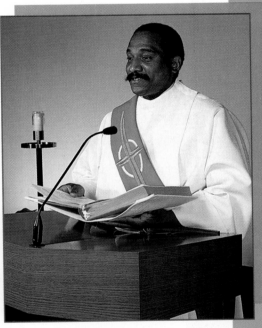

▲ A deacon reads the gospel.

As you learn more about God and the Church, you will discover in what special ways God is calling you to be a helper.

▲ A religious sister teaches a class.

ABOUT Religious Sisters

Religious sisters have a special vocation. They are women who live together in groups called communities. Religious sisters spend all of their time working for God's family, the Church.

Some sisters are teachers. They teach in elementary schools, high schools, and colleges. Other sisters work among the poor or in hospitals. Still others are missionaries who bring the good news of the gospel to people in many countries around the world. Religious sisters do the work of the Church in many different ways.

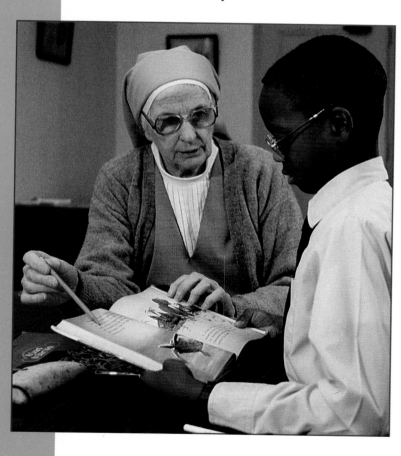

Every sister promises God and the other sisters that she will love God very much. She promises to live her life in a simple way. She hopes that people will see her goodness and try to live a better Christian life.

✿ How Catholics Pray

Prayer is talking to and listening to God. God always hears our prayers. In prayer, we can thank and praise God. We can ask for God's help. We can pray alone or with others. The Mass is our greatest prayer.

ABOUT Kinds of Prayer

We can thank God for our wonderful world.

We can thank God for the gift of our families and friends.

We can ask God's help to live as Jesus taught us.

We can pray at morning and at bedtime.

We can pray with our families at mealtime.

We can pray in school with our teacher and classmates.

At Sunday Mass, we pray with our families and the whole parish community.

ABOUT The Lord's Prayer

Jesus taught his friends **The Lord's Prayer**. All followers of Jesus pray the prayer Jesus taught. In this special prayer, we honor God. We pray that what God wants for us and for all people will be done. We ask God for the things that we need. We ask God to keep us safe from anything that may harm us. Then we pray, "Amen!"

Our Father, who art in heaven, **hallowed** be thy name.

God is our Father. We pray that everyone will remember how good God is.

Thy kingdom come,

Jesus told us about God's kingdom. We pray that everyone will live as Jesus taught us to live.

thy will be done on earth as it is in heaven.

We pray that everyone will obey God's laws.

Give us this day our daily bread;

We know that God cares for us. We pray for our needs and the needs of the poor.

and forgive us our trespasses as we forgive those who trespass against us;

We ask God to forgive us for the wrong things we have done.

and lead us not into temptation,

We ask God to help us always to choose what is right.

but deliver us from evil.

We pray that God will protect us from things that may harm us.

Amen.

Our "Amen" says that this is our prayer, too.

WRITE-IN GLOSSARY

absolution

_____ is the words of forgiveness the priest prays over us in the sacrament of Reconciliation.

Advent

_____ is the time before Christmas when we get ready for Jesus to come into our lives.

altar

An _____ is the table at which the Mass is celebrated.

ambo

An _____ is the reading stand where the word of God is read.

angel

An _____ is a messenger from God.

anointing

_____ means putting blessed oil on a person's body as a sign of love, respect, honor, or healing.

Ash Wednesday

_____ is the first day of Lent.

Baptism
_____ is a sacrament of
welcome. At Baptism, our lives are joined to Jesus and the
Church welcomes us as new members.

baptismal font
A _____ is the water
font where new members of the Church are baptized.

Catholic Church
The _____ is the
Christian community to which we belong.

Catholics
_____ are followers of
Jesus who belong to the Catholic Church.

celebrations
_____ are special times
when we show how important someone or something is to us.

chalice
A _____ is the special
cup that holds the eucharistic wine at Mass.

Christians
_____ are friends and
followers of Jesus Christ.

Christmas
_____ is the time when
we celebrate the birth of Jesus.

parish church
A _____ is a place
where Catholics gather to pray with other members of the
Catholic Church.

Communion

_____ is a part of the
Liturgy of the Eucharist. At Communion, Jesus gives himself to
us in the Eucharist.

community

A _____ is a group of
people who share something important together.

confess

_____ means to tell our
sins to a priest in the sacrament of Reconciliation.

Confirmation

_____ is another
sacrament of welcome into the Catholic Church through which
the Holy Spirit makes us strong to live and share our faith in Jesus.

contrition

_____ means to be sorry.

crucifix

A _____ is a cross that
holds the body of Jesus.

disciples

_____ are persons who
live and love as Jesus did.

Easter

_____ is the time when
we remember and celebrate Jesus' rising to new life.

Emmaus

_____ is the place where
Jesus shared a meal with two of his followers after he rose to
new life.

Eucharist

_____ is Jesus' gift of
himself to us in the Eucharist we receive at Mass.

Eucharistic Prayer The _____
is a special time at Mass for praising and thanking God.

faith

_____ in Jesus means
that we have come to know him and trust him.

fasting

_____ is eating less
food than we usually do.

godparents

_____ are two people
chosen by our parents to help us grow as friends and followers
of Jesus.

Good Friday

_____ is the day when
we remember Jesus' death on the cross.

gospel The _____ is the third
reading we hear at Mass. It tells about Jesus' life and teachings.

grace

_____

- -

_____ is God's loving
presence in our lives.

**Great
Commandment**

_____

- -

The _____
tells us how to show our love for God and our neighbor.

guide

_____

- -

_____ means to show
the way.

hallowed

_____

- -

_____ means holy.

heaven

_____

- -

_____ is unending
happiness with God.

holy

_____

- -

_____ means to be like
God.

Holy Saturday

_____

- -

_____
is the day when we remember that Jesus died to give us new
life. We wait and watch for Jesus' rising to new life.

Holy Spirit

_____

- -

The _____ is the Spirit
of God who helps us follow Jesus.

Holy Thursday

_____

- -

_____ is the day when
we remember Jesus' Last Supper.

Holy Week _____ is the week before Easter.

homily A _____ is a special talk by a priest or deacon that explains the readings we listen to at Mass.

hosts _____ are bread that becomes the Body of Christ at Mass.

lectionary A _____ is the book where all the Bible readings used at Mass are found.

Lent _____ is the time before Easter when we get ready to celebrate Jesus' resurrection.

Liturgy of the Eucharist The _____ is the second part of the Mass. It begins as we prepare to share a special meal with Jesus.

Liturgy of the Word The _____ is the first part of the Mass.

Lord's Prayer The _____ is the prayer that Jesus taught us.

Mass The _____ is a special meal with Jesus. At Mass, we pray together and listen to God's word from the Bible.

missionary

A _____ is a person who tells people about God.

mysteries

The _____ of the Rosary are special things that God has done for us through Jesus and Mary.

New Testament

The _____ is the second section of the Bible. It tells about the life and teachings of Jesus, his disciples, and the first Christians.

Old Testament

The _____ is the first section of the Bible. It tells about God and God's people who lived before Jesus.

parish

_____ is another name for our Christian community.

pastor

A _____ is the leader of a parish.

paten

A _____ is a special plate that holds the eucharistic bread at Mass.

penance

A _____ is a prayer or good action the priest asks of us. Doing a penance shows God that we are sorry and want to be more caring.

Pentecost

_____ is the day when we celebrate the coming of the Holy Spirit. It is the birthday of the Church.

prayer

_____ is talking to and listening to God.

Prayer of the Faithful

The _____ is the last part of the Liturgy of the Word. During this prayer we pray for ourselves and for people everywhere.

presence

_____ means being with someone.

procession

A _____ is people walking in line for a special reason.

reconciliation

_____ means making up and becoming friends again.

respond

_____ means to answer with words or actions.

responsibility

A _____ is something we are supposed to do as members of a community.

responsorial psalm

_____

- -

A _____
is a psalm we use at Mass to respond to God's word.

resurrection

_____

- -

_____ is Jesus' rising
from death to new life.

right

_____

- -

A _____ is something
we deserve to have as human beings.

Rosary

_____

- -

The _____ is a special
prayer that honors Mary.

sacrament of Reconciliation

_____

- -

The _____
is the sacrament in which we say we are sorry for our sins and
celebrate God's forgiveness.

sacrifice

_____

- -

_____ means to give
something out of love.

saint

_____

- -

A _____ is a special
person who shows us how to follow Jesus.

Savior

_____

- -

Jesus, the Son of God, is our _____
who saves us from sin and death.

serve

_____ means to help others and to be kind to them.

seven sacraments

The _____ are special signs and celebrations of Jesus' love for us that make him present to us now.

sin

_____ means to hurt someone on purpose or to do something we know is wrong. When we don't do something we know we should do, we might also sin.

sponsor

A _____ is someone we choose at Confirmation to help us live as a friend and follower of Jesus.

tradition

_____ means doing something the same way every year.

unity

_____ means joined together in peace.

vestments

_____ are special garments worn by the priest during Mass.

worship

_____ is giving honor and praise to God.

CREDITS